⚜A⚜
THRONE
ROOM
VIEW

To Joye —
God Bless you!
Enjoy the view
Lou

Edited by Ric Mandes

ISBN-13: 978-0-9991444-3-5

Printed in USA

Table of Contents

Foreward
BY BILL ISAACS

Matthew 11:28 *(NLT)*
Come to me, all of you who are weary
and carry heavy burdens, and I will give you rest.

Sometimes life is hard. This teaching of Jesus signifies the remedy for today's hectic pace of our daily living and from the constant struggle of our soul. In this context, rest is more than sleep and it is more than escape from the daily grind. Rest is a state of mind, a settled peace that comes from a right relationship to our Father. In such a place, peace can reside while life situations rage!

In 1873, tragedy came to Horatio Spafford when his wife, Anna and their four daughters were crossing the Atlantic while he remained in Chicago to attend to business. A collision with another boat sank the ship the Spafford family was on and took the lives of the four daughters. While on his way to Wales to find his surviving wife, Spafford penned these words to the classic hymn, *It is Well With My Soul*,

> When peace like a river attendeth my way,
> When sorrows like sea billows roll,
> Whatever my lot, Thou hast taught me to say,
> It is well, it is well with my soul.

Life will have its moments and some of them will be tragic and others will be challenging and stressful. It is not the storms of life that define us but how we live and react to them.

From the author's heart of worship and devotion come these powerful moments of "Selah," allowing each of us, as readers, to pause and find refreshment as disciples and believers of Jesus Christ. It has been my joy to have known Janet Swanson and her husband Cary for many years. They are worshippers and they are servants of the God they worship! I'm confident the words you will read are not casually placed on the page but have been wrestled with, lived out and settled in Janet's heart already. Let me encourage you to place this volume beside your Bible, make time on a regular basis and read, reflect and enter into the place of rest that God has offered to each of us.

I commend my good friend on her work and look forward to the future volumes to come!

Bill Isaacs
Lagrange, Ohio
2018

Foreward
BY GARY AND LORI LEWIS

We've come to know Janet in the past two years and upon meeting her an immediate connection formed. God has gifted her with many abilities and she is using them, each time stepping out in obedience. This 21-day devotion book was birthed out of her personal journey.

We've often heard of a "bird's eye view" which means *an elevated **view*** of an object from above, with a perspective as though the observer were a ***bird.*** How much more profound and penetrating is a ***Throne Room View***? Talk about the ultimate elevated view! We can get a completely new perspective on our life's situations by applying scriptural truths that pertain to everyone.

We encourage you to prayerfully read, process and absorb these pages, allowing the Holy Spirit to reveal things you've never seen or thought of before.

Gary and Lori Lewis
South Georgia Administrative Bishop
2018

A Word from the Editor

Janet Swanson's literary work is challenging and intimate for her readers. Her thoughts come off the pages, tough in their formation. Tough in the questions she leaves for you to answer. In my half century of writing and editing, Swanson's work is a delight as she is a master of evocative scripts.

From that evening's altar call, Janet, a damaged teenager opened her heart to the Lord, moved to the high ground and has never looked back.

She is a power point for the Gospel. We feel that in her presence as an Ordained Minister from the pulpit. During a recording session as she lays down musical tracks of God's message. We are taken by her "singing His Word."

Now, this veteran for God presents A THRONE ROOM VIEW. This journey she offers is overwhelming to say the least. Quite amazing as she uses these pages to introduce a spiritual driven offering of a different and a divine place to pray. Readers, all, let me say here and now with no hesitation, Janet's sacred thoughts, touched by the scripture will deepen your commitment to where to PRAY or get you started.

For spiritual growth, find a quiet place and become involved in Janet's offerings.

Ric Mandes
Statesboro, Georgia
2018

Introduction

A Throne Room View is a 21-day in depth study devotion book that will give you a different perspective of life's journey and its challenges it may bring to you. My hope is your life will be changed forever by reading the devotions, the insight and prayers I have written for 21 consecutive days. It takes 21 days to break a habit (old way of thinking) and 3 cycles of 21 days to create a new habit (a new way of thinking).

My prayer is for the first 21 days to set the tone for a prayer life in the throne room and communion with God. During these 21 days, you will be breaking strongholds, old ways of thinking, distorted doctrine, bad habits, pride and insecurity and so much more! Through each devotion you will be inviting the Holy Spirit to be a part of your day and HE will draw you close, teach you, guide you, and convict you to the heart of Jesus. You will find yourself burying an old life style of unbelief, wrong belief and negativity. While embracing a new season, a new you, a new way of thinking, you will see that you now have a habit of coming before the Lord Jesus, in His Throne Room. You will become addicted to His love and His presence and nothing less will do.

I have seen many Christians living out life from Earth to Heaven instead of Heaven to Earth. We have to get the mind of Christ and the view of Christ in order to live a full, abundant and effective life in Christ Jesus.

I pray after 21 intense days of study, devotion, journaling and prayer, you will be living from heaven to earth with a new perspective on life.

Blessings,
Janet Swanson

A Throne Room View

by Janet Swanson

Day 1

Jesus Is the Door

John 10:7-10 (NLV)
*Again, Jesus said to them, "For sure, I tell you, **I am the Door of the sheep.***
All others who came ahead of Me are men who steal and rob. The sheep did not obey them.
*__I am the Door__. Anyone who goes in through Me will be saved from the punishment of sin. He will **go in and out and find food.***
The robber comes only to steal and to kill and to destroy.
__I came so they might have life, a great full life__.

We are living in a time where people are searching for many ways, (many doors) to get to God or to heaven. They are looking for a formula, outside of Jesus Christ, the Son of God, to get to God. But Jesus has made it very clear in the Word of God, that no one can get to the Father without walking through this Door, Jesus.

Notice Jesus said He is the DOOR, and whoever comes to Him, will be saved!

I often remember the thief on the cross who cried out to Jesus from his heart and instantly, was saved. The way we walk through "The Door" is by crying out to Jesus from a sincere heart. All the issues of life are in the heart. *(Proverbs 4:23)* Everything you do in life will stem from the heart. Your walk, your talk, your attitude, your clothing, your hair style etc.

All addictions are rooted in lack of love. Lack of love comes from a belief system started in the heart. People are going through the motions of life and living on an empty tank. Jesus said to us while we are here on earth we can have an abundant life.

John 10:10 says the thief (the enemy, the devil) comes to KILL, STEAL & DESTROY, but JESUS has come to give us LIFE and life more ABUNDANT.

In abundance there is no lack! That's why the Psalmist David penned in the **23rd Psalm**, "The Lord is my Shepherd, I SHALL NOT WANT." Well, what does that mean? It means I am full, I have no lack, I am content, I am happy, I am blessed. It means Jesus will supply all your needs.

When you give your life to Jesus and you walk through "The Door," He said you will go IN & OUT and find food. Well, what does that mean? It means, when you come to Jesus, on a regular basis, you will never leave His presence on EMPTY! He will feed you, and guide you, direct your footsteps, give you wisdom and insight for living, speak to you about the truth, show you mysteries, enable you to believe, help you be strong, He will enable you to do the impossible! When you accept Jesus in your heart, you walk through the door, but it's not the last time you walk through it. You will come to Him on a regular basis. Just as you eat a well-rounded meal, three times a day, in the same way, you need to take spiritual food from the Throne Room of heaven, so your spiritual life can be nourished and sustained.

It is God's will for you to come to Him for all your needs. But not just in your time of need, HE wants to commune with you on a daily basis. He wants to show you things that will prevent unnecessary pain in your life. He wants to help your marriage! He wants to help you raise your children! He wants to help you find your spouse! He wants to help you make money! He wants to help you find your career! He wants to help you find peace, joy and happiness!

Look at this! In **1 Thessalonians 5:23** it says God wants to make you WHOLE in spirit, soul and body! You are made up of all three! So many people leave the spirit out of their daily lives and they look for other doors to walk in because they feel a void in their life. The Bible says He has given to every human on the planet a measure of faith (Romans, Ephesians). He has put eternity in every heart (Ecclesiastes). But look how Paul explained our life lived out before the Lord in Romans!

> **Romans 12:3** *(MSG)*
> *I'm speaking to you out of deep gratitude for all that God*
> *has given me, and especially as I have responsibilities*
> *in relation to you. Living then, as every one of you does,*
> *in pure grace, it's important that you not misinterpret*
> *yourselves as people who are bringing this goodness to*
> *God. No, God brings it all to you. The only accurate way*
> *to understand ourselves is by what God is and by what he*
> *does for us, not by what we are and what we do for him.*

Isn't this powerful? See, Paul was going in and out of that Door finding food for his soul. He lived from a higher place! That is exactly what you and I need to do! It's not by what we do, or what we can give to Jesus, but it's all about who Jesus is for you and wants to give you while you are here on earth! He wants to fill you up on a daily basis. When you come to His table you will never lack for anything.

In **Psalm 23** it says He prepares a table for you in the presence of your enemies.

In the Book of Isaiah it says there is no weapon the enemy can form that will prosper!

> **Isaiah 54:17** *(NKJV)*
> *No weapon formed against you shall prosper, and every*
> *tongue which rises against you in judgment You (the*
> *Lord your God) shall condemn. this is the heritage of the*
> *servants of the Lord, and their righteousness is from Me,"*
> *says the Lord.*

God never said the weapon wouldn't form, but He did say it wouldn't prosper. God is in charge of the people who condemn you. There are no formulas. All we have to do is lean in towards Jesus. Keep our eyes upon Him. Know the Door of Heaven is ALWAYS open, and you can walk through it and find food. You will find truth, you will find wisdom, you will find creativity, you will find blessings, you will find prosperity, you will find inventions, you will find gifts, you will find peace and so much more.

You don't have to look any further! The Throne Room of Heaven has ALL you need.

We are living in times where people are in search of spiritual things and unfortunately there are people who are offering peace, prosperity that is not attached to the True Vine, the True Door, Jesus.

Recently, someone suggested a book for me to read. It looked okay to me on the outside. As I opened the cover and begin to explore the book, I saw where a lot of churches had used some of the "formulas" in this book to achieve success.

The terminology used in this book was the "Law of Attraction." Basically, whatever you dwell on is what you attract. It made a lot of sense to me as I read it. I had heard different pastors in the past say, "familiar spirits attract." There is an old saying that, "the birds of a feather flock together." Which it means those of similar taste congregate in groups. Well, there isn't anything that really sounds "wrong" about that. It is true. But the more I began to read the book, the redder flags that went up. Even though I read scripture in this book, the name of Jesus was never mentioned except for one time and it was used in a mocking kind of way.

Later I found out that this book was based on "New Age" beliefs. She referred to "God" as the "Universe" and "we" (humans) as "creators." And the Universe serves us like a Genie. This book pointed to a truth but twisted with a lie. And it bothered me even more that millions of people had read it and believed it. The body of the book is: you attract what you think on and the universe will be glad to give you whatever you think on. A twisted truth. Just like the devil desires. To twist the truth.

When you believe in God the Creator of the Heavens and the Earth, the Universe and everything in it, and Jesus the son of God, He didn't die upon the cross just to grant us wishes. But He died to give us eternal life, healing, joy, peace, prosperity, abundant life, a full life and a healthy mind, spirit, soul, and body!

The Author teaches and wants prosperity, without Jesus, she wants happiness without Jesus, she wants love, without Jesus, she wants healing without Jesus, she wants heaven, again, without Jesus. She would rather have the feeling of the *"**Power of Attraction**"* rather than the feeling of the *"**Power of the Holy Spirit**."* It is the Holy Spirit that bears witness to Jesus and points to Jesus, whereas this book points to absolutely nothing except to one's self.

Again, Jesus said, "I am the Door." He said, "I am the Way, the Truth and the Life." He said no man could get to the Father without walking through the Door. He also said He came to give us life, and life more abundantly while we are living right here on earth. Well, how do we get that? Having the mind of Christ, the heart of God and the sensitivity of the Holy Spirit will teach you all things, to understand the mystery and feel the heartbeat of God.

The only way you can get that is by accepting Jesus Christ as your Savior, by walking through the Door that will give you life eternal, and life more abundantly here on Earth.

> When you accept Him, you can walk through that Door, straight to His **Throne Room** and will give you a brand-new perspective on life.

Notice in *John 10:9* it says, "**I am the Door.** Anyone who goes in through Me will be saved from the punishment of sin. He will **go in and out and find food**."

Do you see that? He said when we walk through that door, we will go **IN** and **OUT**. That means I can have communion with Him (Jesus and the Father). I will find whatever I need right there in His Throne Room. While I am living here on Earth, I can go in and out on a regular basis. This was the price Jesus Christ paid for us. He is the DOOR. There is no other way to enter in the kingdom of God.

When you walk through that door, you are walking with Jesus. The Word says you will go in and out of that door. There is a door in the tabernacle of heaven and the door is open. Jesus is open to you. He wants you to come to Him and you will find everything you are looking for. You will be full. But that's not all. You will find what you need when you come in and you will carry it with you when you go out. In essence, this is what it means. When I pray, I am entering through the DOOR, Jesus. I am coming to His Throne Room with my request, and I am leaving the Throne Room with an answer. When I go in I will find HIM, Jesus, when I go out, I will carry HIM, Jesus, with me everywhere I go. Jesus is everything you need. When you find Him, your search is over for someone to fill the voids in your life. No matter how many motivational speakers you come in contact with, or how many books you may read on how to grow rich, there is none who can compare to Jesus and the Words He speaks over your life.

We need to concentrate on WHO is the center of my life? Where have I put Jesus?

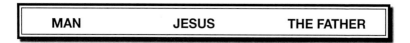

| MAN | JESUS | THE FATHER |

Look at this! When God sees YOU (man), He sees you through Jesus. Jesus represents You before the Father. He's the DOOR! No man can come to the Father unless he comes through Jesus first.

Look at these scriptures very carefully with me:

> **John 14:6-9** (NLV)
> Jesus said, "I am the Way and the Truth and the Life. **No one can go to the Father except by Me**. If you had known Me, you would know My Father also. From now on you know Him and have seen Him."
> Philip said to Jesus, "Lord, show us the Father. That is all we ask." Jesus said to him, "Have I been with you all this time and you do not know Me yet? **Whoever has seen Me, has seen the Father.** How can you say, 'Show us the Father'?

Jesus is letting them know He is perfectly representing God the Father on earth. He is the "skin" of God. He is the "arms" of God. He is the "voice" of God. He is saying, "when you see ME, you have seen God."

After He died on the cross, He rose from the grave in 3 days and then was seated at the right hand of the Father. The Bible says now, He is pleading our case before the Father. Imagine that! When we pray, our prayers are going through Jesus and He is carrying our prayers to the Father!

> **1 John 2:1-2**
> *My dear children, I am writing this to you so that you will not sin. But if anyone does sin, we have **an advocate** who pleads our case before the Father. He is Jesus Christ, the one who is truly righteous. He himself is the sacrifice that atones for our sins—and not only our sins but the sins of all the world.*

This is why He said you will go **IN** and **OUT** and find FOOD! That means when you come to Jesus, there will be no lack in your soul. No voids! You must come into a personal relationship with Jesus. Not religion! Not just going to church but becoming the church. Then you will go OUT and be the hands and feet of Jesus.

My son, Reed Swanson, taught a lesson on Jesus being the Middle Man! He said this: "Jesus is the middle man. The church has put the pull-pit as the middle man. The worship team and band have put their talent and microphones as the middle man. We must put Jesus back in HIS proper place. Your talent must not be placed as the door to God. But Jesus is the Door to God. The pull-pit is there to draw men unto Jesus, to walk through the door to meet with Jesus Christ. Your talent is there to draw people to Jesus through worship. Preaching, singing, and playing your instrument is not the door to God, but it is the door to man to see Jesus. Jesus is the door!"

Prayer:
Father,
I come to You, in the name of Jesus. The most powerful name of all. I recognize there is no other God before You. None can compare to You. You are the God who created the heavens and the earth and everything in it. You are Majestic and Glorious, All-Knowing, All-Powerful, Almighty, Omnipresent, True and Pure. Jesus, I recognize and declare You are the Door, You are the Way, You are the Truth and You are the LIFE and I accept **all** of Who You are! Your Word says I am Yours and You are mine. Thank you, Jesus, for dying for me, for loving me so much You willingly laid down

Your life for me. If I were the only one You had to lay Your life down for, I know You would do it for me. I thank You for loving me Jesus. So, now I come to You, boldly! I come boldly to Your Throne Room. Your Word says I can go in and out and I will find food. I recognize in Your presence there is FULLNESS of joy! I WILL BE FULL! I lay down in this very moment all my needs, concerns, questions, doubts, disappointments, and failures, and I will leave Your Throne Room with a brand-new prospective of who You are and who I am in YOU! Lord, I worship and love You with all my heart, my soul and my mind. I love You with my life. Come and fill me now with Your sweet Holy Spirit and teach me Your ways and bless me oh Lord. I give myself completely to You. In Jesus Name I pray, Amen!

PERSONAL THOUGHTS

_____

_____

_____

_____

_____

_____

_____

_____

_____

_____

_____

_____

_____

_____

_____

_____

_____

_____

The Earth is My Footstool

> *Isaiah 66:1 (NLV)*
> *The Lord says, "**Heaven is My throne**, and the **earth** is*
> *the place where I **rest My feet** (a footstool). Where then is*
> *a house you could build for Me? And where is a place that*
> *I may rest?*

Notice the difference between the statement and the question God is implying here. First, He says, "heaven is My throne room and earth is the place I rest my feet." Then He asked two questions, "Where is a house you could build for Me and where can I find rest in this house?"

Basically, the Lord is saying, "I want to have a relationship with you. I want heaven to invade earth. I want to find My place in the tabernacle of your heart. I want to find my place in your church, in a cooperate place of worship, as well as your private place of worship. I want to be welcomed!"

> *2 Chronicles 16:9 (NKJV)*
> *For the eyes of the Lord run to and fro throughout*
> *the whole earth, to show Himself strong on behalf*
> *of those whose heart is loyal to Him*

See, His eyes are searching the whole earth *(his footstool)*, looking for someone who is ready for God to show Himself strong on their behalf. And while He is doing that, He calls it "rest." The Earth Is His Footstool!

> *Acts 7:49 (NKJV)*
> *Heaven is My throne, **and earth is My footstool**.*
> *What house will you build for Me? says the Lord, or*
> *what is the place of My rest?*

Think about it just a minute. It is our feet that carry us everywhere we go. When our feet hurt, our entire body hurts, and when our entire body hurts, our feet do not want to carry us anywhere. We just want to find a place to rest our feet. That is a fact! But not God! His feet never get weary or tired. His place of rest refers to His "dwelling place." This is the place where He wants to meet with us and commune with us!

> As ironic as it is, the word "foot" or "feet"
> carry so many different idioms.

For Example:

- If I am paying for my child's education, it means that I am to **"foot the bill."**

- When a bride or groom is having second thoughts about the wedding, it is said they have **"cold feet."**

- When a man is said to have **"feet of clay,"** it is acknowledged that he is fallible.

- To be on a **"firm footing"** is to enjoy a stable position as in business or a personal relationship.

- If we **"get off on the wrong foot"** we are placed in an unfavorable position.

- An employee who is **"given the foot/boot"** is FIRED!

- Someone who **"plays footsie"** with another person or a given situation is having an intimate relationship, perhaps flirting with disaster.

- Someone who is **"foot loose,"** however, is just gone wild.

- If we **"put our foot in our mouth,"** (*I have done this a few times)* we blunder by making an embarrassing or troublesome remark.

- **"Putting one's best foot forward"** signifies doing his/her best.

- To **"put one's feet to something"** is to act on the basis of prior information or convictions.

- **"Getting a foothold"** on a problem secures a firm basis for solving it.

- If we **"put our foot down,"** we make a firm decision (*usually with our kids*) with regard to something or someone.

- To **"follow in one's footsteps"** is to emulate another's example or occupy his/her former position.

- To **"leave one's footprints"** is to provide an example or an impression.

The Word says to not let the devil get a "foothold."

One day I was in prayer, and this was one of those moments where I had a visitation from the Lord. After prayer, I laid in my bed and fell asleep. I felt an angel of the Lord come by bedside and he took me to the third heaven. Perhaps I was dreaming. As Paul said, whether I was in body or out of body, I really do not know. *(2 Corinthians 12:2)* I saw a door and Jesus was standing there and I saw His loving hand reach out to me. As I stepped inside the door, I found myself at the Throne Room of Heaven.

I was amazed! The love I felt when I walked in was indescribable. I felt like a beautiful bride and my Groom was holding the hand of my heart and speaking gently, softly, kindly, but powerfully to my soul. I felt as if I were going to melt! I saw pure light. The light was so bright there was no shadow in His presence. Everything was exposed. His glory, His love, His kindness, His peace, His joy, His laughter, and His power were revealed to me in a way I had never seen. There were no words spoken, but much was said!

I only moved when He moved, and I only went where He led me. Then He showed me a place that was literally, "out of this world"! I saw Power sitting on the Throne!

It was God, I could not see His face. Jesus was leading me to the chair He had saved for me, beside Him. As He led me, He caused my eyes to look down at the throne room floor. I had never seen anything so amazing, so beautiful. Nothing compares to this floor. It was as a crystal ocean that I could stand on. I felt like I was walking on diamonds. It was crystal clear, and crystal clean. I saw squares all throughout the floor, (like a princess cut diamond).

Then, Jesus touched my eyes and suddenly my vision was enlarged, and

I saw what He was seeing. Jesus fixed my eyes on a certain square that represented a particular country in the World. I zoomed in on this country. It looked as if I were in Africa. Then I felt His love for Africa and the people there. My heart was deeply in love with these people as I felt the heart of Jesus. Then we zoomed closer! I saw a church worshipping Jesus in Spirit and truth and He said, "this is my resting place!"

He was so happy to be welcomed in His own house built for Him! Then we zoomed in closer and I saw a woman on her knees crying out to Jesus to save her son! She was weeping! I felt overwhelmed to the point of tears! I could feel that Jesus was weeping too! But then quickly He moved my eyes to where her boy was. His eyes were upon the boy of whom his mother was praying! I saw Him breathing upon the boy!

Then, He moved my eyes back to the throne. He pointed to another square, and He took my eyes to this country, it was the U.S.A. Again, He showed me the churches where He was welcome, and He showed me the men, women and children who were calling upon the name of the Lord. I saw Him touching them with His breath as He breathed upon them from the Throne Room.

He smiled at me and said, with no words, just an inner knowing that He was speaking to my spirit, "Heaven is my Throne and Earth is my Foot-stool. Where is the place I can find my rest? Who is the person who has their heart open to Me? To whom can I reveal My secrets to?

He saw the Earth through the Throne Room Floor, which was His foot-stool. His eyes were in search of a hungry heart that was crying out to Him.

It was the coolest thing ever!

- God did not have His **"foot in His mouth"** where He regrets anything He has ever said.
- Nor did He get up on the **"wrong foot,"** God is not grumpy or in a bad mood.
- God does not have **"feet of clay,"** where He in fallible!
- Neither does He have **"cold feet,"** He never has seconds thoughts about His promises and His love towards us. He is committed to us. He has paid the price! Jesus!

- He has **"foot the bill"!** He got a **"foothold"** on sin, once and for all!
- He put His **"best foot forward"** by becoming flesh.
- He **"put His foot down,"** to death, hell, and the grave! He made a firm decision with regard to His beloved bride, His church, His people!
- He definitely "**left His footprints**" upon this earth and made a deep impression of His love towards mankind by sending Jesus and revealing His precious love towards us!

God's feet do not become tired or weary where He has to rest them. No! But quite the contrary! He never gets sleepy! He never has to take a nap! He never gets tired, confused or frustrated. But He is strong and mighty in battle. And even in battle… He is resting!!! What a sobering thought!

**Heaven is His throne
and Earth is His footstool.**

This is about worship and relationship from Heaven to Earth. David knew it best! This is how David worshipped God!

> **Psalm 132:7** *(NKJV)*
> *Let us go into His **tabernacle** (throne room); Let us worship at His footstool (from Earth).*

Prayer, worship and communion happen from **Heaven to Earth**. While you are in the throne room the bible says you can bind things on earth and it will be bound in heaven. Also, you can loosen things in earth and it will be loosened in heaven. The New Life Version puts it this way:

> **Matthew 18:18-19** *(NLV)*
> *"For sure, I tell you, whatever you bind (do not allow) on earth will be bound in heaven (not allowed in heaven). Whatever you loosen (allow) on earth will be loosened (will be allowed) in heaven. Again I tell you this: If two of you agree on earth about anything you **pray** for, it will be done for you by **My Father in heaven**.*

Our prayers are powerful. Our tongue is powerful! The Bible warns us about taking oaths in the Throne Room! Look at what Jesus said here:

> **Matthew 5:33-35** *(NLV)*
> *"You have heard that it was said long ago, 'You must not make a promise you cannot keep. You must carry out your promises to the Lord.' I tell you, do not use strong words when you make a promise. Do not promise by **heaven.** It is the place where **God is.** Do not promise by **earth.** It is where He **rests His feet.**"*

Look where Jesus is!

> **Hebrews 1:13** *(NLT)*
> *And God never said to any of the angels:*
> *"Sit in the place of honor at my **right hand** until I humble your enemies, making them a **footstool** under your feet."*

Look where we are!

> **Ephesians 2:6** *(NKJV)*
> *...and raised us up together, and made us sit together in the **heavenly places** in Christ Jesus...*

Look where John went!

> **Revelation 1:17** *(NKJV)*
> *And when I saw Him, I fell at **His feet** as dead. But He laid His right hand on me, saying to me, "Do not be afraid; I am the First and the Last.*

Where are Feet of Jesus? THE EARTH!

Prayer:

Dear Heavenly Father, Abba God,

I come to You in the name of Jesus. I thank You for Your Word! Thank you, Jesus for giving us access to the throne room. Thank you for Your blood that tore the veil and opened the door of heaven, so we can go in and out anytime our hearts desire. Today Father, I declare my heart will be Your tabernacle and Your resting place. Come dwell with me. Father, I want You, I love You and I need Your presence in my life. You are my Abba Father, my Daddy God and I long for your warm embrace and Your powerful touch. All the days of my life Lord, may my house, where I dwell, have Your footprints. May the house where You want to meet with us have Your Footstool pulled out for you! We want You to be in our churches as You have already said in Your Word, "I am in the MIDDLE of My church!"

Now Father, I come in agreement with Your Word over my life! I bind every foul, evil spirit that is working against me, my family, my community, my country and my church. I loosen every blessing and gift you have for me, my family, my community, my country and my church. I receive the gift of healing and miracles right now. Lord, I know you want to bless me and my family. I speak life over them. I speak life over my situation. I pray for a mighty, outpouring of Your spirit over this generation! Reveal Yourself to us! We want to see Your glory, Lord. Lay Your hands upon me and bless me in my dwelling places. Now, Lord, since Your feet are resting upon my heart, may my feet rest in this city, state, and country, where I trod and everywhere my feet are planted! Your Word says everywhere my feet go, I will possess the land. In Jesus Name I pray, I believe it and I receive it! Amen!

⟡ PERSONAL THOUGHTS ⟡

_____

_____

_____

_____

_____

_____

Day 3

Set Your Thoughts Above

Colossians 3:1-4 *(MSG)*
So, if you're serious about living this new resurrection life with Christ, act like it. Pursue the things over which Christ presides. Don't shuffle along, eyes to the ground, absorbed with the things right in front of you. Look up and be alert to what is going on around Christ — that's where the action is. See things from his perspective. Your old life is dead. Your new life, which is your real life — even though invisible to spectators — is with Christ in God. He is your life. When Christ (your real life, remember) shows up again on this earth, you'll show up, too — the real you, the glorious you. Meanwhile, be content with obscurity, like Christ.

I love the way the Message Bible puts it. Literally, what he is saying is don't go around your whole life with a negative outlook on life. Your life is precious because Jesus is your life. You have a hope! You have an advocate! You have a seat saved for you where Jesus Christ is. When you become a new creation in Christ, you have a brand-new outlook. You have a different view from the world now. You have the best seat!

Have you ever been to a concert, or a basketball game and you had the worst seat? I remember one time we went to a Brave's Game in Atlanta, Ga. We sat in the nose bleed section. I told my husband, "We could've had a better view from the hotel room watching TV than from here!" But, you know what? For a little extra money, we could have gotten a seat up front and have a full view of what was going on!

Jesus has paid a high price for your seat! You have the best seat in the Throne Room. You are seated with Christ Jesus!

Ephesians 2:4-9 *(NIV)*
*But because of his great love for us, God, who is rich in
mercy, made us alive with Christ even when we were dead
in transgressions—it is by grace you have been saved.
And God raised us up with Christ and* **seated** *us with him
in the heavenly realms in Christ Jesus, in order that in the
coming ages he might show the incomparable riches of
his grace, expressed in his kindness to us in Christ Jesus.
For it is by grace you have been saved, through faith—and
this is not from yourselves, it is the gift of God—not by
works, so that no one can boast.*

We have been raised up and made alive with Christ Jesus. The Word also says He wants to SHOW us the incomparable riches of His grace and kindness. Jesus is kind and loving! When you have the right perspective from above, you will see and experience the kindness Jesus, the person. Jesus is calling us to a higher place. He doesn't want us to go there on occasion, but He wants us to live from there. God knows our life will follow our thoughts, so we need to get the mind of Christ. Have you ever heard the saying, "They are so heavenly minded they are no earthly good"?

To be heavenly minded is to have the **mind of Christ.** Then we are to work out the plans He has for us HERE on Earth! Jesus said we ought to pray God's will to be done here on Earth as it is in heaven. Well, how do you know what the plan of heaven is if you never take your thoughts up? The Word says we are to set our thoughts on things above.

1 Corinthians 2:15-16 *(NLT)*
*Those who are spiritual can evaluate all things, but they
themselves cannot be evaluated by others. For, "Who can
know the Lord's thoughts?
Who knows enough to teach Him?" But we understand
these things,* **_for we have the mind of Christ_**.

To have the mind of Christ is to be heavenly minded.

Did you know you can have the mind of Christ? But… before you have the mind of Christ, you have got to change your mind! You've got to renew your mind!

> **Romans 12:2**
> *Do not conform to the pattern of this world but be transformed by the renewing of your mind. Then you will be able to test and approve what God's will is—his good, pleasing and perfect will.*

To be transformed is to be radically changed! That's what Jesus does! Everything He touches He changes!

Have you ever been around someone who was continually negative? Can you feel their energy when they walk in the room? A person who is chronically negative will carry around a weight, a heaviness that will beam from their heart, severally feet away, you will pick up on it before they even open their mouth to say a word. Why is that?

It's because their thoughts have become their identity. And their identity flows from the heart. Their thoughts are always negative. They always see the glass half empty rather than half full. They always see the bad before they see the good.

In the same way, when a person who is full of exuberant life, joy, and happiness and they enter the room, you can feel the energy he or she carries. It makes you feel happy to be around them. You may even find yourself smiling for no reason at all.

To have a negative spirit is one who is a carrier of bad news, they would rather talk about bad news than to talk about any news at all, especially the good news!

> **1 Corinthians 15:1-2**
> *Now, brothers and sisters, I want you to **remember the Good News** I told you. You **received that Good News message,** and you continue to **base your life on it**. That Good News, the message you heard from me, is God's way to save you. But you must continue believing it. If you don't, you believed for nothing.*

Now Paul is encouraging us to receive the good news, to dwell on it, and to base our life on it. When you base your life off the "Good News" you will become a carrier of the Good News! What is the Good News? JESUS!

Whatever you dwell on (in thoughts) is what you will believe. Your behavior follows what you believe. Your life will follow your behavior.

You may be asking, well, how do I break the pattern of "negative thinking"?

I'm so glad you asked! I am going to give you some tools to use in your everyday walk with the Lord that will help you.

- Realize you cannot do it within yourself. You have to yield your heart to Jesus and the work He wants to do in you. So, the first thing you have to do is DIE TO SELF! The Holy Spirit is here on Earth to HELP YOU, and Jesus is seated at the right hand of the Father and He is calling you to come up higher! A higher way of thinking, a higher way of walking, a higher way of speaking, and a higher way of living. You have to crucify the flesh before you can enter into the Throne Room of God. And the Holy Spirit is here to help you **DIE TO SELF**.

  Galatians 2:20

- You have to realize, to think on things negative, is to carry on a conversation with hell itself. To think on things positive is to carry on a conversation with heaven. You get to choose to whom you want to speak. When hell starts speaking to you, you have to recognize WHERE it is coming from and then you CAST IT DOWN. So, the second thing you have to do is to **CAST DOWN IMAGINATIONS**. Train your brain to recognize when you are getting negative. You will know it because if you ask the Holy Spirit to help you, He will bring back to your remembrance all things. Cast every negative thought down. Take it into captivity and make it come in obedience to the mind of Christ.

  2 Corinthians 10:5

- You have to realize it is God who gave you such a vivid imagination. Let's look at this word for a moment. Imagination comes from the word "Imagine." The root word of "Imagine" come from "Image." Remember this: God created us in His IMAGE. The Hebrew word for Image is HEART! Isn't that so cool? Look at this: God carried you in HIS heart. He saw you with His imagination from His own likeness and then He made you! He said it was good! So, thirdly, to think as Christ, is use your **IMAGINATION for GOOD**!

Remember what the word says in *Eph. 3:20* "I will do exceedingly above what you can think, comprehend or imagine."

Focus on what is good! **Look** for what is good! **Seek** for what is good! Instead of trying to find something wrong, try to find what is right.

Let's take a look at what the Word of God has to say about these things.

> *Philippians 4:8 (NKJV)*
> *Finally, brethren, whatever things are true, whatever things are noble, whatever things are just, whatever things are pure, whatever things are lovely, whatever things are of good report, if there is any virtue and if there is anything praiseworthy—meditate on these things.*

To meditate means to actually imagine them. In other words, imagine the best, imagine a good report, imagine things that are praise worthy. When you are carrying on a conversation with heaven, (The Throne Room) you are hearing the heart of Jesus. Now, let's take a look in the Word again!

> *Colossians 3:1-4*
> *Since, then, you have been **raised with Christ, set your heart on things above**, where Christ is, seated at the right hand of God. Set your mind on things above, not on earthly things. For you died, and your life is now hidden with Christ in God. When Christ, who is your life, appears, then you also will appear with him in glory...*

Did you see that? SET YOUR HEART on things ABOVE...

When you set your heart on things above, there is no telling what will come out of heaven for your life. God's dreams for you are bigger than your own. He has a magnificent plan for you!

Look at this!

On Aug. 28, 1963, the Rev. Martin Luther King Jr. delivered his "I Have a Dream" speech from the steps of the Lincoln Memorial.

Where do you think his "dream" came from? It came from time of being with the Lord, in the Throne Room of God. He knew how to cast down negative imaginations about his situation and his people. God spoke to his heart and gave him a dream. He saw it with his imagination. My friends, to dream is to imagine! In the same way that God saw YOU in His heart, then made you. You have to imagine your dream in your heart! Then it will come to pass!

Look what came from Martin Luther King Jr. as he dreamed, as he imagined freedom!

> *"I say to you today, my friends, that in spite of the difficulties and frustrations of the moment, I still have a dream."*
> **Martin Luther King, Jr.**

> *"Now is the time to rise from the dark and desolate valley of segregation to the sunlit path of racial justice"*
> **Martin Luther King, Jr.**

> *"I have a dream that my four little children will one day live in a nation where they will not be judged by the color of their skin but by the content of their character."*
> **Martin Luther King, Jr.**

> *"I have a dream that one day this nation will rise up and live out the true meaning of its creed - we hold these truths to be self-evident: that all men are created equal."*
> **Martin Luther King, Jr**

"Let us not seek to satisfy our thirst for freedom by drinking from the cup of bitterness and hatred."
Martin Luther King, Jr.

"I have a dream that one day on the red hills of Georgia the sons of former slaves and the sons of former slave-owners will be able to sit down together at a table of brotherhood."
Martin Luther King, Jr.

Ladies and gentlemen, where do you think his dream came from?

<u>His Imagination!</u>

Where do you think he got that? It came from the Throne Room of God, from the heart of God for His people.

God gave "the dream" to Martin Luther King Jr. because he was spending time with HIM in prayer, worship and communion. He believed God and literally took HIM for His Word when He said:

> **Ephesians 3:20-21**
> *Now to Him (Jesus) who is able to do exceedingly abundantly above all that **we ask** or **think**, (imagine or dream) according to the power (Holy Spirit Power) that works in us, to Him **(Jesus)** be glory in the church by Christ Jesus to all generations, forever and ever. Amen.*

Will you take God for real? Who do you want to have conversation? And from where do you want your dreams and ideas to be birthed? Having conversation with heaven or with hell?

I want to encourage you to **"set your thoughts above!"** You are in Christ, seated at the right hand of the Father. You have been granted access to the Throne Room of God! Set your heart above, as the Father pours His dreams into your heart. Then, and only then, can you carry out HIS perfect will on this earth and will accomplish great and mighty things.

Prayer:

Dear Abba Father,

I come boldly to your throne room, knowing that I am accepted by You. Father, I ask that You fill me with Your dreams. Give me eyes to see through Your eyes. Give me ears to hear what You are saying to me. Give me courage to walk out the dreams You have for me. Lord, help me on a daily basis to see the possibilities of each day instead of focusing on the challenges of the day. Help me see from a brand-new perspective. From my earthly view, things look so distorted. But from Your throne room, I can see clearly because in the light of your presence there is no shadow. There is no darkness to distort the truth. I yield my heart to You, Jesus. I choose to think on the good things. I choose to crucify my flesh. I choose to trust You, even though I may not see it, I know that You are working. You are a Promise Keeper and a Miracle Worker. You will not fail me. You will not let me down. Lord, I want my conversation to be with You and for my thoughts to be pure. Create in me a clean heart and show me my evil ways. Heal me of my woundedness. I come to Your throne room and I make an exchange. I trade my doubt for belief, my anger for comfort, my negativity for positivity, my bitterness for contentment and my unforgiveness for forgiveness. I ask You to renew a right spirit within me, in Jesus Name. I believe I have what I ask for. Therefore, I know You will respond to me with loving kindness. I am Yours and You are mine my Lord. I love You, Jesus. I thank You for looking past my faults and seeing my needs. You are filling every void in my heart right now with Your sweet love. I receive ALL You have for me, in Jesus name. Amen!

PERSONAL THOUGHTS

Day 4

Come Up Here

Revelation 4:1-11 (NKJV)
*After these things I looked, and behold, a **door standing** open in heaven. And the first voice which I heard was like a trumpet speaking with me, saying, "**Come up here**, and **I will show you things** which must take place after this."*

*Immediately I was in the Spirit; and behold, **a throne set in heaven**, and One sat on the throne. And He who sat there was like a jasper and a sardius stone in appearance; and there was a rainbow around the throne, in appearance like an emerald. Around the throne were twenty-four thrones, and on the thrones I saw twenty-four elders sitting, clothed in white robes; and they had crowns of gold on their heads. And from the throne proceeded lightnings, thunderings, and voices. Seven lamps of fire were burning before the throne, which are the seven Spirits of God. Before the **throne there was** a sea of glass, like crystal. And in the midst of the **throne**, and around the **throne**, were four living creatures full of eyes in front and in back. The first living creature was like a lion, the second living creature like a calf, the third living creature had a face like a man, and the fourth living creature was like a flying eagle. The four living creatures, each having six wings, were full of eyes around and within. And they do not rest day or night, saying:*
"Holy, holy, holy,
Lord God Almighty,
Who was and is and is to come!"
Whenever the living creatures give glory and honor and

*thanks to Him who sits on the **throne**, who lives forever
and ever, the twenty-four elders fall down before Him who
sits on the **throne and worship Him** who lives forever and
ever, **and cast their crowns before the throne, saying:**
"You are worthy, O Lord, to receive glory and honor and
power; For You created all things, and by Your will they
exist and were created."*

Before we can understand this well, let's first take a look at *Rev. 1*.

Revelation 1:9-11
*I, John, both your brother and companion in the tribulation
and kingdom and patience of Jesus Christ, was on the
island that is called Patmos for the word of God and for
the testimony of Jesus Christ. <u>I was in the Spirit on the
Lord's Day,</u> and I **heard behind me a loud voice,** as of a
trumpet, saying, "I am the Alpha and the Omega, the First
and the Last," and, **"What you see, write in a book** and
send it to the seven churches which are in Asia:*

Let's look at some of the key words here.

- I was in the spirit on the Lord's Day
- I heard a voice from behind me
- Write in a book what you see and send it to the churches

It's important to see John on an Island by himself because of the Word of
God and the Testimony of Jesus Christ. He honored the Lord by continual
prayer and worship. Worship was his thing. He was caught up in the Spirit.
He was in worship and prayer. His body was on the earth, but his heart
and imagination (mind) were on Jesus. Maybe he was thinking on the
Word of God and the scripture then he heard a voice behind him.

Isaiah 30:21 (NKJV)
*Your ears shall hear a word behind you, saying, "This is
the way, walk in it," Whenever you turn to the right hand or
whenever you turn to the left.*

John heard a voice behind him saying, "I am the Alpha and Omega… write down what you see, then send it…

Now, let's look at **Rev. 4**

We already know John was in the Spirit and it was on the Lord's Day. And we know he heard the voice of Jesus. Now, Jesus is about to show him something like he had never seen before. Notice what happened next.

- He saw a door **OPEN** in heaven, then he heard a voice say, "**come up here**, I want to show you some things… "

Jesus did not go down to where John was, but He was petitioning John to COME UP to where He was! Jesus was calling John to **Come UP higher!!**

> **Isaiah 55:8-9** *(NIV)*
> *"For my thoughts are not your thoughts, neither are your ways my ways," declares the Lord. "As the heavens are higher than the earth,*
> *so are **my ways higher than your ways** and my thoughts than your thoughts."*

If you are interested in learning the thoughts of Jesus, then you have to go **UP**. His thoughts are **HIGHER** than our thoughts. His WAYS are **HIGHER** than our ways. In order to hear from heaven, we must **GO UP**!

Our Lord is always interested in our GOING UP and not TURNING BACK. When you turn back, all you see is your past, the regret, shame guilt and pain from your past. Remember what happened to Lot's wife when she looked back? She turned into a pillar of salt. Imagine that! I know we are supposed to be the salt and light of the world **(Matthew 5:13-16)**, but our salt doesn't come from looking back, it comes from the harmonious flavor of our dear Lord Jesus Christ. For the Word says in **Psalm 34:8**, " *O Taste and see that the Lord is good!"*

When you are going up, the Lord will show you "things to come."

So many times, when we pray we are asking Jesus to come and help us. We ask Him to show us His glory, down here, to meet us where we are, down here. This is not a bad thing, but it is imperative to know and understand what the Holy Spirit is!

The Holy Spirit is down here on Earth helping us. When we are talking with Jesus, we must go UP where He is. We must take our thoughts higher! We must take our worship higher! We must take our prayers higher!

If you read carefully, you will see and feel the atmosphere of heaven. John saw there was a throne, and there was someone sitting on the throne. God! You will see the 24 elders, which some theologians believe are the 12 tribes of Israel, and the 12 disciples. You will see the beast with eyes all over them (*nothing catches God by surprise)* who are constantly pacing between heaven and earth. They never get tired or sleepy! They never need a nap!

They were all worshipping the Lord. The atmosphere is lit! That's what my children would say! It is illuminated. There is no darkness. There are no shadows. There is no sickness. There is no depression. There is no hate. There is no conflict. There is no pain. There is no foggy brain! Remember what Jesus said, "Let Your will be done on earth as it is in heaven." The Lord was showing John His will. Then John was to carry it out, here on the Earth! You cannot carry out God's will for your life with fog in your brain! You need to try to think about how you think, and how you pray! And make a clear assumption of where your thoughts are coming from. Discern the thought, then go UP to the Throne Room of God. This is what John did!

Nothing has changed. Still today, Jesus is calling for us to **come up higher**. We must go to the throne room and worship, pray, talk, commune, dream, and finally, to make the great exchange in order to carry out the will of God in our life. The great exchange is trading in your sorrow for joy, sickness for healing, discouragement for courage, your weakness for strength! Whatever is negative, and weighing you down, you can trade it for the complete opposite at the Throne Room of God.

John's body was still on the earth, but Jesus took his imagination **UP**! He was in a trance. His total mind (heart) was captivated by the power of Jesus. This is how prayer should be. This is how worship should be. This is how our church services should be.

When we are in worship, we should be **GOING UP!** When we are praying, we should be **GOING UP**! When we are listening to our preacher, we should be **GOING UP**!

Finally, notice this! "… they cast their crowns at His feet… ." In other words, where there is TRUE worship, and prayer, there is a "casting" that takes place. Maybe you need to "cast your cares" or maybe you need to "cast away pride & envy" or maybe you need to "cast away fear and worry," or maybe you need to "cast down imaginations that exalt itself against God," or maybe you need to "cast your net" to the other side to see what God is doing. And you will definitely have to "cast away your flesh." Crucify that stuff. Get a new perspective at the *Throne Room* of God. The *Throne Room* of God is pure and holy. If you will **"COME UP,"** He is faithful to show you all the things as you ask Him. He is faithful to meet you in the *Throne Room*. God wants to meet with you. He longs for you to talk with Him. He desires for you to take some time out of your busy schedule and spend some time with Him. He wants to give you ideas for work. He wants to inspire you to write a song. He wants to preach a message through you. He wants to help you start that new business. To all the men, He wants to give you an understanding of your wife! And wife, He wants to give you an understanding of your husband. And to parents, He wants to show you the heart of your teenager! You will find all this and so much more as you take your thoughts UP! Take your prayers UP! Take your worship UP! As you begin to do this, and you open your heart to imagine God seated on His Throne and Jesus is at the right hand of the Father, and you imagine yourself in His presence, you will begin to see life from a whole other perspective.

Make this your first priority. God loves having the first part of your day. He loves to meet with you in the morning time. When you meet with Him in the morning, it sets the tone for your day. You will see that you will be more kind, more patient, more understanding, more loving and more Christlike throughout the day. You will find you are viewing things from a higher perspective and will become more positive and optimistic about your circumstances.

> "There is but one good; that is God. Everything else is good when it looks to Him and bad when it turns from Him."
>
> **C.S. Lewis**

As the old saying goes… Keep looking up! Keep your chin up!! Things will get better! To keep your chin up is to say, Lord, I will lift my eyes to the hills, where I know my help comes from. I look to You Lord.

Make a date with the Lord each day. Plan on getting up 30 minutes earlier than you usually do. Put on your favorite praise & worship music. Or just sit quietly and listen to the sound of quietness. It's a beautiful sound. The morning is filled with glory and splendor. There is a certain sound of the morning you do not get at any other time throughout the day. It is fresh! The Word says His mercy is new every morning.

There is Joy in the Fellowship of God

> **Psalm 63** *(NKJV)*
> *(A Psalm of David when he was in the wilderness of Judah.)*
> *O God, You are my God; **Early will I seek You**; My soul thirsts for You;*
> *My flesh longs for You In a dry and thirsty land Where there is no water.*
> *So I have **looked for You in the sanctuary**, To see Your power and Your glory.*
> *Because Your lovingkindness is better than life, My lips shall praise You.*
> *Thus I will bless You while I live; I will lift up my hands in Your name.*
> *My soul shall be **satisfied** as with [marrow and fatness, And my mouth shall praise You with joyful lips.*
> *When I remember You on my bed, **I meditate on You in the night watches**. Because You have been my help, Therefore in the shadow of Your wings I will rejoice. My soul follows close behind You; Your right hand upholds me.*

As you see in this Psalm, David is seeking the Lord **EARLY** and he medi-ates at night as he lays his head down to sleep. In between the morning and night, David is looking and searching and praising God and blessing God and speaking words of life over his day! Take the time to say this prayer out loud then write down your own thoughts and requests you have for Lord. Make today personal between you and Jesus. Make a personal exchange! Take your thoughts UP!

Prayer:

Dear Jesus,

Thank You for Your presence in my life. Thank you for taking me to a high-er place with You. I am so glad to do life with You, Jesus. You make life worth living. With you, I can do anything! Father, I pray that You help me to stay encouraged and focused by remaining in a safe place at your *Throne Room*. I come before Your presence with thanksgiving my Lord. I cast all my cares upon You. I know You care for me. I know You are for me. You are faithful to speak to me and show me the mystery of Your Word. You comfort me, and You prepare a table before me. You lead me and guide me in all truth. Show me Your ways oh Lord. Show me Your glory! Your Word says in Psalms the path of life leads *upward* for the wise that he may keep away from Sheol below. So, I come **upward** to view life here on earth by Your heavenly perspective. I trust You Jesus. You guide me with your eye. Your light has risen upon me. Your hand is upon me. You are my strong and might tower. You are a place of refuge. You are my strength when I am weak. You are my Healer, Almighty Physician! You give me wise counsel. You will never fail me. I make a bold declaration to the spirit realm, there is NOTHING too hard for my God! I believe all things are pos-sible! I praise You oh God for there is a miracle in the making for me today! I praise You for You are a very present HELP in time of trouble. You will cause my enemies to fall for Your Word says every word spoken against me, YOU will condemn! Father help me to STAY HERE, upward with You. In Jesus name I pray. Amen

PERSONAL THOUGHTS

Day 5

The Promise of Rest

Hebrews 4: 1,11,16 (NKJV)
*Therefore, since a promise remains of **entering His***
***rest**, let us fear lest any of you seem to have come*
*short of it. **Let us therefore be diligent to enter that***
***rest**, lest anyone fall according to the same example*
*of disobedience. Let us **therefore come boldly to the***
***throne of grace**, that we may obtain mercy and find grace*
***to help in time of need**.*

My husband and I are pastors of a growing, thriving, multi-cultural church. We see the church in such a beautiful position to reach the lost and to heal the broken. Often, I find myself in a place of "unrest" as we are working diligently for the Lord. It seems as though there are not enough days in the week to do everything I need to do. Then one day, I was so weary and so tired, I heard the sweet whisper of the Lord say to me, "you need to rest, this is not a suggestion, it is a command or else you will be in disobedience." I was like... wow... God! This hit me pretty strong. I thought I was obeying the Lord. I thought I was doing everything He wanted me to do. Or was I doing everything everybody else wanted me to do?

I had to take some time to figure out what "rest" looked like. And when could I take a whole day to rest from all my work and just enjoy the day. I am the type of person where I like to be busy doing something. I had to discipline myself to do something on my "sabbath" that was fun, and not work! Even though my work is fun to me, it was still work and it was stressful.

Exodus 20:8-10 (NLV)
"Remember the Day of Rest, to keep it holy. Six days you
will do all your work. But the seventh day is a Day of Rest
to the Lord your God.

What does **REST** look like to you?

Rest is something Jesus has promised us. And the secret to this is to make the effort to "enter in" to HIS rest. It's not just a physical rest, but it is a "inner" rest. Free from anxiety, worry, fear, frustration and torture! It is to be completely immersed in peace that comes from above. Rest opens the door for HELP in the time of need.

There have been times in my life where the opportunity to become stressed and overwhelmed would come my way. Have you ever had one of those days where it seemed like when it rains, it pours? Well, I certainly have. Just yesterday! While I was studying on "rest" the opportunity came my way to be stressed, fearful, worried and afraid.

It was strange to me the same thing was happening to my husband. My husband is a very gifted man. He's an amazing preacher, pastor, husband, father and my best friend. But he has another gift of seeing what no one else can see. He's a detailed man. He is gifted in taking older homes and turning them into a masterpiece!

We are in the middle of remodeling an older home and we had to do some extensive work on it. He has worked so hard to get it finished, where he has not really RESTED at all. Then to top it off, the painter decides to walk out on the job and leave us hanging. He became overwhelmed, stressed and anxious. Then he stepped out of the house to go and pray. He called on the HELPER! Yes, he needed help with the house, but he needed more help with what was happening on the inside. He had to make the effort to **enter in** to rest and not to be worried or anxious.

At the same time, I received some strange mail that would suggest a stalker. The mail has been coming for almost a year now, and I don't know who it is. But it sent cold chills up and down my spine. I immediately came OUT of REST and into fear and worry. I lost my breath as I opened a card and a package. Tears shot out of my eyes, then I remembered the word I had been studying. **Rest**!

How can a person rest when you are faced with fear, abandonment, debt, lack, anxiety and worry?

Well, I am telling you what I had to tell myself. Breath deep, close your eyes, and make the effort to enter the *Throne Room* of grace. I have to remember what the Word says, "I will find help in the time of need." **Psalm 46:1**

Then I was reminded of what the Lord had showed me a few days before all this happened. I got up that morning to pray and while I was at the *Throne Room* praying, I saw two angels beside me. The Lord said to me, "I have assigned these two angels over you to protect you. Nothing will come near to you to harm you."

It was just one of those days it seemed everything was going wrong. I felt afraid, stripped, and alone. But then Jesus walks in the doors of my heart as I made the effort to reach out to Him, and He consoled me and gave me peace, and rest.

> *Fear had no choice but to leave while*
> *I was in the Throne Room of Grace!*

It requires trust in order to enter into rest. It took me about one full hour of "diligently" entering into "His" rest in order to feel at peace. Fear had no choice but to leave while I was in the *Throne Room* of Grace. I felt it when it lifted off of me. I kept saying to myself, "I will not fear! If God is for me, then who can be against me! God has not given me the spirit of fear, but of love, power and a sound mind. The angels of the Lord are encamped all around me. I will only see with my eyes a thousand to fall at one side and ten thousand to fall at the other side."

Ask yourself this, "what is keeping me from being at peace and being at rest on the inside?" When you enter the *Throne Room* of Grace, remember what has been keeping you from rest and inward peace, then lay it at the feet of Jesus and find grace, peace, joy, and rest for your weary soul.

Give your heart time to understand what God is doing!
Janet Swanson
A word from Abba Father, to my heart

Sometimes we have to sit back and give our heart time to understand what God is doing. Everyday fear will raise its ugly head in some shape, form or fashion. You will have the great opportunity to be afraid, perhaps on a daily basis. But at the same time, you have the great opportunity to believe God for a miracle and divine protection and provision. When the enemy comes in like a flood, God will raise a standard against him. This standard is rest! Be assured of this one thing. God is fighting your battles. He wants you to trust Him and remain at peace, and rest.

When things get hectic, chaotic and crazy, take a moment to step away from the situation and look at it from the lenses of God. The closer you are to the problem, the bigger it seems. But if you step away from it, the smaller it looks. For example, when you are getting ready for a long trip, you will drive to the airport to catch a plane. When you approach the plane, it looks so big and monstrous. But the further it gets in the air, the smaller the plane looks. It's the same for the person who is in the plane. The further you get away from the ground, the smaller everything looks. Here is the fact. Nothing changed. The size of the plane didn't change, but our perspective of the plane changed depending on where we were viewing it from.

Our peace and rest are found in the Throne Room of God. It's a high place! A place of security and peace. Sometimes we need to take a step back, breath deep, refocus, and take our problems up before the Lord. You know what? It really boils down to trust! Father, do I trust YOU? When you trust the Father is at work on your behalf, you will be at rest in the middle of the fire!

Look at this story!

Daniel 3
King Nebuchadnezzar made a gold statue ninety feet tall
and nine feet wide and set it up on the plain of Dura in

the province of Babylon. Then he sent messages to the high officers, officials, governors, advisers, treasurers, judges, magistrates, and all the provincial officials to come to the dedication of the statue he had set up. So all these officials came and stood before the statue King Nebuchadnezzar had set up.

Then a herald shouted out, "People of all races and nations and languages, listen to the king's command! When you hear the sound of the horn, flute, zither, lyre, harp, pipes, and other musical instruments, bow to the ground to worship King Nebuchadnezzar's gold statue. Anyone who refuses to obey will immediately be thrown into a blazing furnace."

So at the sound of the musical instruments, all the people, whatever their race or nation or language, bowed to the ground and worshiped the gold statue that King Nebuchadnezzar had set up.

But some of the astrologers went to the king and informed on the Jews. They said to King Nebuchadnezzar, "Long live the king! You issued a decree requiring all the people to bow down and worship the gold statue when they hear the sound of the horn, flute, zither, lyre, harp, pipes, and other musical instruments. That decree also states that those who refuse to obey must be thrown into a blazing furnace. But there are some Jews—Shadrach, Meshach, and Abednego—whom you have put in charge of the province of Babylon. They pay no attention to you, Your Majesty. They refuse to serve your gods and do not worship the gold statue you have set up."

Then Nebuchadnezzar flew into a rage and ordered that Shadrach, Meshach, and Abednego be brought before him. When they were brought in, Nebuchadnezzar said to them, "Is it true, Shadrach, Meshach, and Abednego, that you refuse to serve my gods or to worship the gold statue I have set up? I will give you one more chance to bow down and worship the statue I have made when you hear

*the sound of the musical instruments. But if you refuse,
you will be thrown immediately into the blazing furnace.
And then what god will be able to rescue you from my
power?"*

*Shadrach, Meshach, and Abednego replied, "O
Nebuchadnezzar, we do not need to defend ourselves
before you. If we are thrown into the blazing furnace, the
God whom we serve is able to save us. He will rescue us
from your power, Your Majesty. But even if he doesn't, we
want to make it clear to you, Your Majesty, that we will
never serve your gods or worship the gold statue you have
set up.*

There are some things the enemy is shouting at you. There are some things he is demanding from you. His roar has haunted you. His threats have tortured you. He wants you to believe a lie. He is telling you to fear. He is telling you to worry. He is telling you that you are never going to get ahead. He is telling you that you are not worthy to be a Christian. The Devil is a liar and he is the father of lies. There is no truth in him and he is shouting to you to bow down to fear, to bow down to worry, to bow down to anxiety, to bow down to unforgiveness, to bow down to hate, to bow down to become a victim!

Shadrach, Meshach, and Abednego know exactly how you feel. They too heard the roar! They heard the shout from the enemy to bow down! The world wanted them to conform to their ways, but these boys refused. These boys were at perfect peace. I don't know about you, but there is something super scary about being burned alive! This is what the enemy wants to do to you and me. He wants to burn us alive to death! But there was something going on in the heart of these three boys! There was a trust that God would not fail them. Even to the point of, "If He doesn't deliver us, we still will not bow." There was a powerful trust so deep in their soul that nothing could take it away. They believe God and trusted Him even unto the fire! They had seen HIM come through time after time. But they left the results to HIM. They did not manipulate God. They did not accuse God. They simply trusted God. It was their trust that put them at perfect peace. But God was faithful. Look at the rest of the story!

*Nebuchadnezzar was so furious with Shadrach, Meshach,
and Abednego that his face became distorted with rage.
He commanded that the furnace be heated seven times
hotter than usual. Then he ordered some of the strongest
men of his army to bind Shadrach, Meshach, and
Abednego and throw them into the blazing furnace. So
they tied them up and threw them into the furnace, fully
dressed in their pants, turbans, robes, and other garments.
And because the king, in his anger, had demanded such
a hot fire in the furnace, the flames killed the soldiers as
they threw the three men in. So Shadrach, Meshach, and
Abednego, securely tied, fell into the roaring flames.
But suddenly, Nebuchadnezzar jumped up in amazement
and exclaimed to his advisers, "Didn't we tie up three men
and throw them into the furnace?"
"Yes, Your Majesty, we certainly did," they replied.
"Look!" Nebuchadnezzar shouted. "I see four men,
unbound, walking around in the fire unharmed! And the
fourth looks like a god!"
Then Nebuchadnezzar came as close as he could to the
door of the flaming furnace and shouted: "Shadrach,
Meshach, and Abednego, servants of the Most High God,
come out! Come here!"*

So Shadrach, Meshach, and Abednego stepped out of the fire. Then the
high officers, officials, governors, and advisers crowded around them and
saw that the fire had not touched them. Not a hair on their heads was
singed, and their clothing was not scorched. They didn't even smell of
smoke!

This is what the Lord wants to do for you. He is faithful. He will deliver you.
He will not fail you. The enemy may roar, but Jesus is the true Lion and His
roar is greater than the enemy. Trust HIM with your life. Trust HIM with your
circumstances. Trust Him with your marriage and your finances. Trust Him
with your children. Trust Him with the results that He is at work and He will
not fail. Trust the fact that Jesus loves you more than you could ever imagine. You have to make the effort to enter into REST and not WORRY!

Let's take another look at what rest looks like!

Hebrews 4: 1,11,16 (NKJV)
*Therefore, since a promise remains of **entering His** ***rest**, let us fear lest any of you seem to have come short of it. **Let us therefore be diligent to enter that rest**, lest anyone fall according to the same example of disobedience. Let us **therefore come boldly to the throne of grace**, that we may obtain mercy and find grace **to help in time of need.***

Prayer:

Dear Lord Jesus,

You know the pain we carry in this world. You know the anxiety we can carry around. You know how the enemy is roaring in our ear. You know what it feels like to suffer, to be in pain, to be sick, to feel anxiety, worry and every other emotion one carries on this earth. When You died on the cross, You felt it all. You felt the solitude, the pain, rejection, abandonment, abuse, and death. Not only did you die, but you died "death." You went to the depths in order to free me. I can boldly come to You knowing You are very well acquainted with my grief and pain. Also knowing that You are great and mighty, and you are at work on my behalf. You were in the furnace before the three Hebrew boys were! You were on the other side of the roar and was there to deliver them. So, now I come boldly to your Throne of Grace to receive REST, to receive peace. I believe with all my heart that you will deliver me. Father, I make the exchange today in Your *Throne Room*. I will give You my fear, for love, anxiety for peace, sadness for joy, mourning for dancing, worry for REST. Even though I don't un-derstand what my heart is feeling, You do! You understand me! I will not fear! I will trust in You! I will not worry! I will trust You! I will not give in to the roar of the world, I will trust You. I will not be transformed to what the world wants of me. But I will be transformed by the renewing of my mind knowing You love me. Right now, Your precious love is covering me like a blanket. I receive Your grace, Your love, and Your power to overcome this world. You said, since You have already overcome this world, then so can I! You have made me more than a conqueror. I am strong when I am weak! I trust You are at work even when I don't see it. You are working all things together for my good, and I will not fear. I enter into Your perfect REST! You are in the middle of my chaos. You are in the middle of my pain. You are in the middle of my fire. I declare that I am coming out of this fiery furnace and I won't even smell like smoke or even have a hair on my head burnt! In Jesus name I pray! I declare and I believe it! Amen!

PERSONAL THOUGHTS

Day 6

Worship In The Throne Room

John 4:24 (NKJV)
God is *Spirit, and those who worship Him must worship in spirit and truth."*

Jesus said, "Let thy will be done here on earth as it is in heaven."

Let's put in the word "Worship" where "Will" is.

> **Let Worship be done here on earth as it is in heaven!**

What does worship look like in heaven? I learned from a dear friend of mine, Larry Napier, that the ultimate worship scene in the bible took place in Revelation 5. I would like for you to take the time and let's read about worship in heaven.

Revelation 5:1-3 (NKJV)
And I saw in the right hand of Him (The Father) <u>who sat on the throne a scroll written inside and on the back, sealed with seven seals</u>. Then I saw a <u>strong angel</u> proclaiming with a loud voice, "<u>Who is worthy</u> to open the scroll and to loose its seals?" And no one in heaven or on the earth or under the earth was able to open the scroll, or to look at it.

- Notice here, there is no one who is worthy in heaven, or on earth, or under the earth, those who have died in the Lord to open the scroll.

- Notice who is sitting on the throne and what is in His right hand.

- Notice the Word said that a "strong angel" proclaimed with a loud voice

> *So I wept much, because <u>no one was found worthy</u> to open and read the scroll, or to look at it. But one of the elders said to me, "Do not weep. Behold, the Lion of the tribe of Judah, the Root of David, has prevailed to open the scroll and to loose its seven seals."*
>
> *And I looked, and behold, in the midst of the throne and of the four living creatures, and in the midst of the elders, stood a <u>Lamb</u> as though it had been <u>slain</u>, having seven horns and seven eyes, which are the seven Spirits of God sent out into all the <u>earth</u>. Then He (the lamb, Jesus) came and took the scroll out of the right hand of Him (God) who sat on the throne.*
>
> *Now when He had taken the scroll, the four living creatures and the twenty-four elders <u>fell down before the Lamb</u>, each having a harp, and golden bowls full of incense, which are the prayers of the saints. And they sang a new song, saying:*
> *"You are worthy to take the scroll,*
> *And to open its seals;*
> *For You were slain,*
> *And have redeemed us to God by Your blood*
> *Out of every tribe and tongue and people and nation,*
> *And have made us kings and priests to our God;*
> *And we shall reign on the earth."*

- Notice **who** was in the middle of the throne and the four living creatures

- Notice where the 7 spirits of God is sent out

- Take a moment and think about how the earth has 7 continents and the Lamb has 7 horns and 7 eyes, which are the 7 spirits of God.

- Notice how all of heaven cried out for the one who is worthy… the lamb of God! Jesus!

- Notice the four living creatures and the twenty-four elders, what did they do?

- Notice how the they were playing the harp, offering prayer from the saints, and they sang a new song

- Notice what the new song sounded like and what they sang about: They sang about who was Worthy, who was slain, redeemed by the blood, for all people on the earth, and how we will reign on earth

Then I looked, and I heard the voice of many angels around the throne, the living creatures, and the elders; and the number of them was ten thousand times ten thousand, and thousands of thousands, saying with a loud voice:

"Worthy is the Lamb who was slain
To receive power and riches and wisdom,
And strength and honor and glory and blessing!"

And every creature which is in heaven and on the earth and under the earth and such as are in the sea, and all that are in them, I heard saying:

"Blessing and honor and glory and power
Be to Him who sits on the throne,
And to the Lamb, forever and ever!"

Then the four living creatures said, "Amen!" And the twenty-four elders fell down and worshiped Him who lives forever and ever.

- Notice how many angels were around the throne and what they were saying

- Notice what every creature on heaven and earth and under the earth were saying

- Notice how the living creatures kept falling down at the feet of Jesus and worshipping Him

I wonder how different our church services would be if we would match the kind of worship that is taking place in heaven?

I wonder how different our praise team and choirs would sing if we all matched the sound that is coming from heaven?

I wonder how different our musicians would play if we knew how we ushered the prayers of the saints to heaven?

I wonder how different our prayer life would be at home if we would but match the ultimate worship scene in heaven?

True worship comes out of an encounter with Jesus. True worship comes from the love we have for Jesus. True worship must take place from heaven to earth. We must take our worship UP to the *Throne Room* of God. It is totally possible to go to church and never enter in to HIS presence. Remember what the Word says!

James 4:8
"Draw near to ME, and I will draw near to you."

We must make the effort to go to where HE is! We go there to experience the fullness of His presence. You will know it when you get there! It's powerful!

In your next worship service, when you enter the doors of the sanctuary, say outload, "Lord, I thank You and praise You for all you've done... ." Enter into His gates with thanksgiving.

Psalm 100:4 (KJV)
Enter into his gates with thanksgiving, and into his courts with praise: be thankful unto him, and bless his name.

Then as you are looking for your seat and being social with the people all around you, start bringing all scattered thoughts together. Get your heart, your mind, your thoughts on one page. Then when the worship begins, start mediating on the words of the song. Draw an image of what the song is saying. For instance, if the song is "Every Praise Is To Our God" and you get to the part that says, "God my Savior, God my healer, God my deliver, yes He is, yes He is." Begin to imagine Jesus being all these things to you. Your healer, your deliver and savior. Then before you know it, you will be so focused on Jesus that you are not even aware of WHO is singing, WHO is beside you, or WHO is distracting you. You are focused. You are in the spirit. Your heart, your mind, your thoughts are visually set on *"Throne Room"* worship! It will transform your worship. It will transform your life. Then, imagine this: Your Pastor starts his sermon and let's say he is teaching about Peter walking on the water. Take your imagination to the scripture. Make the scripture come alive in your heart by opening up your imagination and putting yourself there in the story. Pretty soon, you will see yourself taking steps of faith to walk on water.

We have a lady in our church who was going through a very hard time. She felt so bad that she didn't even think God could or would fulfill her dreams as a music teacher. But she heard my husband teach on how "God is not finished with you, if you can dream it, He will fulfill it!" The more she listened, the more alive she became. She sat in the service and she opened up her imagination (heart) to Jesus and dared to ask HIM if He could use anything to use her. Right then and there she penned a song. Not just a song, but a children's musical came out of that sermon. She called it, "The Leader In Me." She taught it to her kid's choir at school and it was a great success. IT WAS AMAZING. She got a standing ovation and over 200 children sang those songs. Then to top it all off, she was voted teacher of the year! How did that happen? Because she took her worship UP! She took her pain UP! She took her disappointment UP! She took her heart UP! Then she could see Jesus clearer than ever before. Like the old song says, "I can see clearly now the rain is gone."

When church becomes your focus, you lose sight of Jesus. When the song becomes your focus, you lose sight of true worship. It is only when **Jesus** becomes your focus and when HE has your full attention, you will start to experience Him and understand what true worship is all about.

Let's take a look again at this scripture:

> **John 4:24** *(NKJV)*
> *"**God is** Spirit, and those who worship*
> *Him must worship in spirit and truth."*

The woman of Samaria came to draw water, and Jesus was already there. He spoke kindly to her and told her of everything she had ever done and not one time condemned her. She had an encounter with Jesus that led to the ultimate worship/salvation experience. She found the ONE who is Worthy! Then as you begin to read more about her life, she never lost focus of the ONE who is worthy!

> I can always tell which kingdom
> you belong to by your worship.
> - *Darlene Zschech*

Prayer:

Dear Father,

I come before Your presence with honor, and thanksgiving. I praise You Father for You do all things well. Nothing catches You by surprise. You are awesome, magnificent, all powerful and Mighty! You pull down strong holds. You heal the sick. You restore the broken-hearted. You have redeemed us with Your precious blood. You stomp the enemy with your heel. You are making a way where there seems to be no way! As You move in heaven, I pray You move here on earth, our country, our state, our city, our community, our schools, our homes and our churches. I pray for heaven to invade us. A Holy Collision! Let worship, prayer, and preaching be done here on earth as it is in heaven. I declare as the angel did with a loud voice for revival to come to our country! I pray for deliverance to those who are in bondage. You can just say one word and it will be done. Let Your words flow through our hearts. In Your presence there is JOY. I pray that in our worship services people will feel demons leave them, addictions will be broken, tradition will have to bow, and the ultimate worship scene will take place in YOUR HOUSE! I pray we, your sons and daughters, will stay focused on You, and nothing else matters. I pray for a radical people who are not ashamed of the gospel who will stand up and declare You are Worthy to receive all glory, all honor, all praise and all glory. Reveal Yourself to this young generation. Reveal yourself to the young mother and father. Reveal yourself to the middle-aged. Reveal yourself to the older saints who have walked with You for years and years. Reveal yourself to all peoples of the earth. I pray for the movement in heaven to move here among us. I proclaim and shout the name of Jesus from the rooftops. Demons tremble at Your name. Chains are broken at the mention of Your name. The depressed are delivered at the mention of Your name. Jesus! Jesus! I love You! I adore You, I praise You for You are worthy my Lord! My King! My God! My Father! AMEN!

PERSONAL THOUGHTS

Day 7

Pain In Betrayal

Psalm 41:9 (NLT)
Even my best friend, the one I trusted completely, the one
who shared my food, has turned against me.

I wonder who this friend was that David was talking about? Could it have been his best friend Jonathan? Jonathan was the son of King Saul. King Saul hated David and was trying to kill him. When you read the story, put yourself in David's shoes and see if you can feel the pain by becoming a part of his story with your imagination.

This is how it began. This text takes place after David kills Goliath.

1 Samuel 18:1-4 (NKJV)
Now when he had finished speaking to Saul, the soul
of Jonathan was knit to the soul of David, and Jonathan
loved him as his own soul. Saul took him that day and
would not let him go home to his father's house anymore.
Then Jonathan and David made a covenant, because he
loved him as his own soul. And Jonathan took off the robe
that was on him and gave it to David, with his armor, even
to his sword and his bow and his belt.

To me, right away something seems off here. It was only after David was publicly on the scene, killing the giant (that nobody else wanted to face) that Jonathan decides, "Hey, can we be best friends?" Here's my question. Where was Jonathan when David was alone on the back side of the desert? Where was he when David's own father and brothers overlooked him? He was not there. He showed up and wanted to be best friends with David only when a crowd was cheering him on.

Look in *I Samuel 19* where the story goes on. Jonathan says to David, "Hey, I got your back. I am going to take care of everything for you. You stay right here, I will go talk to my father and I will convince him to not kill you." So, David was like, "ok, man. I trust you. You go, and I will stay here and wait." Jonathan goes out and talks his father in bringing David back to the palace. After all, David is his son-in-law. The king's son is David's best friend. King Saul agrees to cease from his anger and to bring David back. But when Saul hears David play the harp, and he hears the crowd cheering David on for all his favor and success, he became jealous and angry. King Saul knew the Lord was with David and His spirit had departed from him. Again, Saul seeks to kill David. So, David runs.

It's humorous to me how every time David hid, Jonathan was the only one who knew where he was. David told him everything. Then it seemed like the next day, King Saul was right there. How else would've King Saul had known?

Have you ever had a friend where you trusted them, you loved them, just to find out their love for you had motives behind it? It seems to me that maybe Jonathan had a motive. When I read the whole story, the friendship of David and Jonathan started off good. But it was always under stress. Jonathan was in a very hard place. He had to choose between his father, who was the king and David, his best friend, who was anointed to be king. Saul knew David would take his place, therefore he wanted to kill him. Nevertheless, Jonathan wavered in the middle and did not make a choice of who's side he was on. In *I Samuel 20*, he told David, "Hey man, I'm going to do these things for you, but if I die, you have to swear forever, that my descendants will sit at the kings table." David swore to him, he made an oath, because the bible says that David loved Jonathan.

But now take a look at David's writings in the Psalms. Take a close look at how he is grieving. His soul is in anguish! See if you can put yourself in his shoes and feel what he is feeling.

> *Psalm 55:11-13 (NLT)*
> *Everything is falling apart; threats and cheating are*
> *rampant in the streets.*
> *It is not an enemy who taunts me— I could bear that.*

It is not my foes who so arrogantly insult me. I could have
hidden from them.
Instead, it is you—my equal, my companion and close
friend.

Wow! Can't you see the betrayal and feel the pain in his words? He said it was not his enemy that was out to get him. We all know that King Saul was his enemy. He said, "I could've hidden from him. But YOU, my friend, my companion, my close friend, my equal, I could not hide from you."

David felt like his life was falling apart because his best friend had a love/hate relationship with him. It was toxic. It was unhealthy. He said that it taunted him. It pained him. His friend insulted him, arrogantly! David expected his enemy to do him harm, but he never expected his best friend to betray him. What David did not realize is that this relationship was TOXIC from the beginning. Let's take a look at a few people in the bible who were betrayed by a friend!

JEREMIAH

Jeremiah 20:10 *(NLT)*

I have heard the many rumors about me. They call me
"The Man Who Lives in Terror." They threaten, "If you
say anything, we will report it." Even my old friends are
watching me, waiting for a fatal slip. "He will trap himself,"
they say, "and then we will get our revenge on him."

JOB

Job 19:19 *(NLT)*

My close friends detest me. Those I loved have turned
against me.

JESUS

Luke 22:21 *(NLT)*

"But here at this table, sitting among us as a friend, is the
man who will betray me."

Wow! Can you see that? Have you ever heard that old saying, "Family is assigned, friends are chosen"? You can't pick your family, but you can pick your friends.

What is a friend? Dictionary.com gives us 3 definitions;

1. a person attached to another by feelings of affection or personal regard.

2. a person who gives assistance; patron; supporter:

3. a person who is on good terms with another; a person who is not hostile:

Friendships are made to bring joy to the heart. Friends are a support, an assistance to one another. Notice that Dictionrary.com says a friend is a person who is NOT hostile. To be hostile is to be warlike, aggressive, adverse, averse, contrary. Hostile, inimical indicate that which characterizes an enemy or something injurious to one›s interests. Hostile applies to the spirit, attitude, or action of an enemy:

Friends are not supposed to be a "dumping area" where you dump all your trash on them. Friends are not manipulative. Friends are not judgmental. Friends are not presuming the worst about one another. Friends are not supposed to feel guilty for having something that the other person doesn't have. Friends are not your friend because of a "title," or "what you can GET out of it.

Look at what the bible says about toxic friendships:

> **1 Corinthians 15:33** *(NLT)*
> *Don't be fooled by those who say such things, for "bad company corrupts good character."*

> **Proverbs 22:24-26** *(NLV)*
> *Do not have anything to do with a man given to anger, or go with a man who has a bad temper. Or you might learn his ways and get yourself into a trap.*
> *Do not be among those who make promises and put themselves up as trust for what others owe.*

> **Proverbs 27:5-6** *(NLV)*
> *Sharp words spoken in the open are better than love that is hidden. The pains given by a friend are faithful, but the*

kisses of one who hates you are false.

I am not trying to scare you away from having friends. But I am asking you to choose your friends carefully. The bible says in order to have a friend, first you must show yourself to be friendly. But even then, he says, even if you do this, your friend may turn from you, but there is a friend who sticks closer than a brother, JESUS!

> **Proverbs 18:24** *(NKJV)*
> *A man who has friends must himself be friendly, but there is a friend who sticks closer than a brother.*

> **John 15:15** *(NLV)*
> *I do not call you servants that I own anymore. A servant does not know what his owner is doing. I call you friends, because I have told you everything I have heard from My Father.*

Jesus calls us His friend. His motives are pure, good and powerful. His intentions are kind towards us. A true sign of a friend is one whom you can talk to and you can tell them anything. Jesus said that he was not withholding anything from us. He is sharing with us everything the Father is telling Him.

Have you ever heard the saying, "you look like you just lost your best friend"?

Have you ever thought about why that saying is so true? Because losing your best friend is like a death. It is painful. It hurts.

But be of good cheer. The Holy Spirit is a comforter. Jesus is your strength. He will pick up all the broken pieces of your life.

> Sometimes walking away has nothing to do with weakness, and everything to do with strength. We walk away not because we want others to realize our worth and value, but because we finally realize our own.
>
> **- *Robert Tew***

There will be times in your life when you will have to walk away from what is toxic in order to survive. In times like this, you will make the *Throne Room of God* your dwelling place. It is a place where you can cry and be real before the Lord. You can tell Him everything you are feeling. And if you let Him, He will even show you the truth about the relationship. He will show you what to do. And there are even times that He will restore what was broken if both sides of the party are repented. But then, there are other times where you will have to give that person completely to Jesus in the *Throne Room!*

Let's go to the Throne Room now. I want you to use your imagination for a moment. Close your eyes and see an open door standing before you. I want you to take the hand of the friend who you feel has betrayed you or hurt you in some way. Walk through the open door with your friend. As a bride would walk down the aisle to meet her betrothed, walk towards Jesus in the *Throne Room.* Take your friend to Jesus and pray this prayer:

Prayer:
Dear Jesus, my Lord and my King,
I come before Your Throne Room with a broken heart. I bring my close friend, my companion with me to make an exchange with You my Lord. Jesus, I now release my friend to You and I pray for her/him. I pray you will fulfill their dreams. I pray You will reveal Yourself to them. I pray You will re-store everything the devil has tried to destroy in their life. I pray for truth to be restored. I pray for honor to be restored. I pray for healing in their heart, soul and mind. I pray blessings upon them. Even though this relationship was too much, it is not too much for you. You can carry the load. You can carry the heaviness. You can take what was toxic and turn it into beauty. I confess with my mouth and believe in my heart that I no longer can carry the pain, torment, and aguish of what is toxic. Even though my heart feels like I have failed somehow, I choose now to put my failures at Your feet.

So, I come to You, and I give it to You! I give my friend over to YOU! And as for me, I ask that You heal my heart. I know you capture every tear I shed. You hear my moaning and groaning. You see the countenance upon my face. You see how my heart has been weighed down with grief. But Your Word has promised to give me beauty for ashes. So, I come! I come to You Jesus. I give You my pain, my disappointment, my guilt, my shame, and my anger to! I confess I will not pick them back up. I pray You create in me a clean heart oh God. Forgive me for putting my complete trust in man. Forgive me for my wrongs I committed that maybe I didn't even see. Show me what is in my heart. Show me how I can improve with my friendships. Lord, I want to have friends, but how can I trust again? You will show me how to trust and who to trust. But YOU, my Lord, are the only one I can truly trust. You will never fail me. I know You want to bless me. I know You are working all things together for my good. You are walking before me. You are my help in times of trouble. You are my hiding place. You are my peace in the midst of the storm. You are my everything. You are my worship and the One I sat my heart upon. I love You Jesus. I thank You for complete restoration. Your Word says In *Joel 2:24-26* that You will make the grain-floors be full of grain again, and the crushing-places will flow over with new wine and oil. You said that you will pay me back for the years that my food was eaten by the flying locust, the jumping locust, the destroying locust, and the chewing locust.

You have a large army which You sent among me. Your angels are encamped all around me! Your Word says that I will have much to eat and be filled. I will have plenty my Lord I will not lack in love. I will not lack in friendships. I will not lack in any area of my life because You are my portion. And I will never cease to praise the name of the Lord my God, Jesus! You have done wonderful things for me. Your Word says I will never be put to shame! Thank You for healing my heart and for healing the heart of my friend. I now leave this in Your Throne Room and I am confident that You will make it right! I trust You Jesus! Amen!

PERSONAL THOUGHTS

Day 8

Letting Go of Anger

Psalm 37:8 *(NKJV)*
Cease from anger, and forsake wrath; Do not fret—it only causes harm.

The Bible says you can be angry and sin not.

Ephesians 4:26 *(TLB)*
If you are angry, don't sin by nursing your grudge. Don't let the sun go down with you still angry—get over it quickly;

Have you ever been so angry that you felt like you were going to blow you top! Anger is a normal emotion. But if left unattended, anger will become a bully! Angry people provoke other people. Anger is rooted in the emotion of being a victim!

I have learned angry boys grow up to be angry men and angry girls grow up to be angry women!

Anger is often caused by wrongs that have been done to us, deep sadness and, most often of all, it's caused by fear. Fear of being out of control, fear of being rejected, fear of being abandoned, fear of being left out and lonely.

Anger is a terrible bully that has a way of pushing its way out to mix in with all your other feelings. It can distort your thinking, your perception and your reality! When you feel the emotion of anger, you need to get a new perspective. You need a Throne Room View to see what has triggered such anger. Because anger not dealt with in a healthy manner will turn into rage.

Stages of Anger:

- Feeling anger
- Thinking anger
- Expressing anger
- Acting anger

The healthiest of these is expressing anger. When you are angry, it is healthy to express it to someone you trust.

If you are being abused, and you are angry about it, your way to freedom is to TELL SOMEBODY!

Your voice is powerful, and you need to use it for the good to bring freedom!

If you fail to express your anger in a healthy way, then you will be forced by emotion to start "acting it" (through insults, threats, sulks, resentments, physical attacks etc) that can become violent and destructive!

Feeling it but not expressing it (or not even realizing you feel it) is repressive and thinking about it but not expressing it can turn to obsession and depression!

The root of depression is pent up anger!

ANGER is a BULLY. Anger will tell you expressing it is not enough. It will either tell you to be quiet and never express it, or it will tell you to express it and do something about it. Anger will tempt you to vindicate yourself. It can cause you to become a bully or become a victim of bullying.

The Word of God says we should never seek to "pay someone back" because of what they have done to us.

> *Romans 12:17-20 (NLT)*
> *Never pay back evil with more evil. Do things in such a way that everyone can see you are honorable. Do all that you can to live in peace with everyone.*

Dear friends, never take revenge. Leave that to the
righteous anger of God. For the Scriptures say,
"I will take revenge; I will pay them back," says the Lord,
Instead,
"If your enemies are hungry, feed them. If they are thirsty,
give them something to drink. In doing this, you will heap
burning coals of shame on their heads"

If you are being bullied or abused, what should you do? How can you walk this scripture out? How do you make peace with a bully or abuser?

You cannot reason with an angry man! When anger is left unchecked by the Holy Spirit, it will open doors for demonic activity. The person may be the one "physically" doing it to you, but it is an evil spirit that is directing that person to such things.

WE MUST PRAY!

You must create a boundary that says, "I will not tolerate this anymore!"

If you are a child being abused by an adult, then you must tell another adult what is happening to you. By this, you are creating boundaries to the spirit world that says, "you cannot cross this line!" But you are also creating a boundary with the ''abuser" that says, "you need to stop, you are hurting me!"

If you are a woman being abused by your husband, you must set a boundary line with this man that says, "If you continue to do this, then I will report you to the police and I will leave you." When you open your mouth and make these kinds of statements, you are doing more than just declaring it to the "abuser," but you are also making a declaration to the spirit world saying, "I will not tolerate this kind of behavior."

If you are being manipulated and abused verbally, then you need to declare, "I will not be verbally abused anymore." You have to create the physical boundary first, then you will see the boundary will be set in the heavens.

The Word says, "whatever you bind on earth shall be bound in heaven! Action must take place on the earth and heaven will respond to your declaration.

At 12 years I cried out to God for the last time before I was about to take my life. I couldn't see a way out. My step-father had been sexually abusing me for 2 years. I was angry. I was a child. I didn't know what to do. But the Lord heard my cry! I made a declaration out loud. I actually kept asking God to kill me! Because I could see no way out. But suddenly, I felt something enter the room, it was peaceful, and I felt it drawing me closer. I remember lying in bed about to overdose on pills, and something drew me to the window. As I looked out the window, I saw the moon in all its glory. It was so big and so close that I felt as if I could reach out and touch it!

It was as if the moon was a spot light upon my room that night. I felt something warm come over me. I felt love enter into my body from the top of my head to the soles of my feet. I heard a voice say to me, not audibly, but deep, down inside my very being, "Don't take your life! I have plans for you! Go back to bed and in the morning, I will tell you what to do."

This is a true story! Then I felt peace come over me. I was not angry anymore. I didn't want to take my life anymore. I almost felt like I floated back to my bed, I felt so light!

This was the one night my step-father did not enter the room to abuse me!

When I woke up the next morning, I still felt peace and I heard the voice again say to me, "Pick up the phone and call the police and tell them what is happening to you, today I will save you!"

So, I picked up the phone and I called the police, I thought for sure when they arrived they would take the bad man to jail. But instead they picked me up and took me away to foster care.

I was confused! I was a child and I had no guidance. No parents! No love! I was angry all over again.

Little by little, God took steps in my life that ultimately led to the woman I am today.

Alone the way, I had to forgive my step-father for abusing me. I had to forgive my mother for giving me up and not believing me when I told her what he was doing to me. I had to STOP BEING ANGRY, and I had to TURN FROM MY RAGE, it was only leading the way of destruction in my life. Rage only leads to harm.

Somewhere and someone how, you have got to be able to say, "Lord, I trust You with the story line of my life. I trust the next chapter will be better. I trust the best is yet to come for me."

When you LET GO OF ALL ANGER (that leads to rage), you will then loosen bitterness and unforgiveness in your life. Then heaven will respond to you and give you peace. Jesus will give you BEAUTY FOR ASHES. He has promised to take what the devil meant for harm and use it for your good!!!

My step-father was a bully! And he was being bullied by anger. After I found a "higher perspective" I was able to see truth and was able to LET IT GO! I now have the "mind of Christ" when I am in the Throne Room of God, seeing from HIS eyes!

When you are truly a victim and you see no way out, **PRAY**, and turn to your community for help. You can turn to your neighbor, an aunt or uncle, a pastor, teacher or principal. You can reach out to your community and tell somebody. Your voice is powerful, and you need to tell somebody what you are going through. You might just tell the right person and they will find a solution for you.

> With every problem there is a solution,
> but there cannot be a solution without a problem!
> *- unknown author*

The solution begins with adults teaching and mentoring our kids on how to express anger in a healthy way. There is an old African Proverb that says, "It takes a village to raise a child."

The village is a community of people. We are a community! Our church is a community. We all need to become a mentor and learn how to speak life into our children and this upcoming generation. We need to teach them by example, and by word!

I used to tell my children when they were younger, when they would get so angry, to go outside and run around the house 3 or 4 times until it subsides. Find a way to release your anger! I heard of one man who says when he gets angry he will lay down.

Whether he is at work, at home, or a ball game, he found it hard to stay angry when he lies down. Maybe you can write in your journal, exercise, or lay down, or play an instrument, write a song, build something, etc. Then when that emotion has subsided a bit you can now exercise forgiveness and **let go** of all anger!

Anger left unattended will turn into a monster. Don't pent it up, and don't let it out of control. But you must find an outlet and go to the Father and make an exchange in the Throne Room of Heaven.

Remember, it is not a sin to be angry! You can be angry without sinning. But it's when you hold on to anger, sun set after sun set, then it begins to fester. It will turn into poison and eventually become your bully and your prison!

Try to settle it! Try to make peace if at all possible. If not, then go to someone you trust to help you. If you cannot settle it or make peace, you have done all you can do and now the Father in heaven is responsible for the rest. Not YOU or ME!

Your freedom awaits you!

The word says, to do good to those who do you wrong. At the same time, if you are being mistreated, abused sexually, physically or verbally, you must not let "anger" take place in your heart or keep silent and pent up all that anger and pain inside of you. It will only lead to depression, sickness and rage. Depression and rage will lead you to harm yourself or someone else. Eventually, your body will start to respond to bitterness.

Create your boundary line and DO NOT allow the abuse anymore.

Prayer:

Dear Father,

I come before your throne room today with all my pent-up anger and rage. I release to You, my Lord, the person who has offended me, abused me, or done me wrong. I choose to forgive them and let go of all my anger. I will not let the sun go down today without releasing to You, all my pain, all my anger, all my frustrations, all my questions of "why me?" and all my brokenness! Lord, I am angry, and I admit that I am! But also, I admit that I need You right now to help me not to pick this back up. Anger is not who You say I am. But I am at peace with the story line of my life. I trust You Jesus to work out every detail for my good. I believe that You have good things for me. I now, make this exchange at Your feet Jesus. I exchange anger for **peace**, revenge for **Your vengeance**, pain for **healing**, disappointment for a **divine appointment**, hate for **love**, and bitterness for **forgiveness**! I declare to the spirit world that I am not a victim, but I am a victor! I declare that I am now free from all retaliation! I declare boundaries lines to be set in the spirit world that no demon can cross over to influence my soul to respond from an earthy view. But I set my heart on things above, I am drawn to Jesus and His precious love! Thank You Jesus for taking all my anger away. Thank you for taking all my pain away. Thank You for lifting this heavy load. I put on the garment of praise for the spirit of heaviness! I love You Jesus! I love You with all my heart, all my soul, and with all that I am! I am Yours and You are mine! I receive Your love and Your forgiveness! In Jesus Name, Amen!

PERSONAL THOUGHTS

_____

_____

_____

_____

_____

_____

_____

_____

Day 9

Forgiveness

Ephesians 4:31-32 (NLT)
Get rid of all bitterness, rage, anger, harsh words, and
slander, as well as all types of evil behavior. Instead, be
kind to each other, tenderhearted, forgiving one another,
just as God through Christ has forgiven you.

FORGIVE: Is a verb and requires action

1. to grant pardon for or remission of (an offense, debt, etc.); absolve.

2. to give up all claim on account of; remit (a debt, obligation, etc.).

3. to grant pardon to (a person).

NOTICE in the book of Ephesians Paul is pointing out things we need to get rid of before we can forgive. Bitterness, rage, anger, harsh words, and slander are the words he started with. Paul is not beating around the bush. He says it straight up! Can you imagine if Paul were your pastor? If Paul were your pastor and you went in to his office for counseling and you told him, you were angry at someone because they betrayed you and hurt you and now you just don't know what to do. Paul would say, "OK, GET RID OF IT!" I find that somewhat humorous! I don't know about you, but when someone tells me something like that, I have the tendency to say, "awh, poor thang, well tell me what happened." But not Paul! He just straight up says, "GET RID OF IT!"

If I were to sit down with Paul and give him all the reasons I had to be angry, and why this person did not deserve my forgiveness, I think he would say something like this to me.

Paul: Now, Janet, forgiveness is not an option, it's a commandment and it's not for the other person. It is for you. When you release the other person from the wrongs they have done to you, then you are free from their contamination in you.

Janet: But, Paul, I was raped, they killed my loved one, they deserve death!

Paul: But Jesus told us, if we cannot forgive, we cannot be forgiven. Have you ever committed a sin?

Janet: Yes, but not like that! I have basically been a good person! The wrong was done to me!

Paul: So, now you are the judge of what is good and bad? I, Paul was the worst of sinners! I was a murderer! I was a slanderer! And I did it all in the name of God ignorantly. But one day I was on my high-horse and His powerful light knocked me off my saddle, and it was more than just a body that fell to the ground, but my pride fell down too, my shame slithered off my back, my guilt was catching up with me, but it melted like wax before the presence of Jesus, my whole life changed. See, I know and understand the power of forgiveness because I have been forgiven. I realized the same thing I judged other people for was inside of me! Jesus showed me my own heart and He forgave me so now, I have to forgive others.

Janet: But they took something from me. Something I can't get back. I feel angry and betrayed!

Paul: And that's why you have to get rid of it. If you don't, you will become just like the one who hurt you and your loved one. Yes, what they did was bad, but God is the judge, not you! For your own sake, LET IT GO and FORGIVE.

Janet: But how? How do I let it go? How can I let go of this pain?

Paul: The same way Jesus did. When He died, he felt murder, incest, rape, guilt, addictions, abandonment, pride, arrogance, anger, shame, and so much more!. He died DEATH! And yet He spoke to the Father and said, "forgive them for they know not what they are doing!"

Janet: So, I forgive by saying what Jesus said? "Forgive them for they don't understand what they are doing?"

Paul: YES! Exactly! Jesus is our example. He had an understanding of their hearts. They were deceived by the devil. He knew it was Satan who was instigating the whole thing. The one you want to be angry with is SATAN, not the person! Because Satan is the author of lies, deceit, theft and pain. If you give your pain to Jesus and see through His eyes where you are seated now, the Throne Room of God, you will be able to look and see the truth. Forgiveness is for your own freedom! Let it go and leave all judgments to God! For HE is your vindicator!

I don't know about you, but sometimes I feel just like this. Paul would say to you and to me, "How can I be in Christ and remain in Christ if I am unforgiving, angry and bitter?" You have to understand, if you don't release the judgement and the pain, it will become "who you are." Then, in return, your mouth will start speaking from your heart out of pain and pain will wound and poison other people in your life. The bible says the tongue holds the power of life and death! Paul understood how powerful words are. He even went a step further and said for us to be careful the tone we use when we are talking to people. Are we harsh? Are we bitter? He is saying we must not only put away rage and anger, but the harsh words that lead to rage and anger. He is saying we need to replace those emotions! Look what he said: Instead, be kind to each other, tenderhearted, forgiving one another, just as God through Christ has forgiven you. Just a thought but take a look at this! He said just as God, through Christ has forgiven you, be kind just as HE is kind to you, be tender-hearted just as HE is tenderhearted towards you! It boils down to one thing! THE HEART!

> **Luke 6:44-45** *(NKJV)*
> *For every tree is known by its own fruit. For men do not gather figs from thorns, nor do they gather grapes from a bramble bush. A good man out of the good treasure of his heart brings forth good; and an evil man out of the*

*evil treasure of his heart brings forth evil. For out of **the abundance of the heart his mouth speaks**.*

The question now remains. What is in your heart? Do you find yourself being kinder to a stranger than you are to your own family? Have you lost the art of a child to be "tenderhearted"? Are you making judgements against people? Are you still holding a grudge after all these years? If so, now is the time to let it go.

> I can only have peace of mind only
> when I forgive rather than judge.
>   *- Gerald Jampolsky*

Here are some of the verses I like to turn to for encouragement when I'm struggling with the difficulty of forgiveness.

Ephesians 4:32
Be kind to one another, tenderhearted, forgiving one another, as God in Christ forgave you.

2 Corinthians 2:5-8
Now if anyone has caused pain, he has caused it not to me, but in some measure—not to put it too severely—to all of you. For such a one, this punishment by the majority is enough, so you should rather turn to forgive and comfort him, or he may be overwhelmed by excessive sorrow. So I beg you to reaffirm your love for him."

Colossians 3:13
Bearing with one another and, if one has a complaint against another, forgiving each other; as the Lord has forgiven you, so you also must forgive.

1 Corinthians 13:4-6
Love is patient and kind; love does not envy or boast; it is not arrogant or rude. It does not insist on its own way; it is not irritable or resentful; it does not rejoice at wrongdoing, but rejoices with the truth.

Luke 6:37

Judge not, and you will not be judged; condemn not, and you will not be condemned; forgive, and you will be forgiven;

John 8:7

And as they continued to ask him, he stood up and said to them, "Let him who is without sin among you be the first to throw a stone at her."

Matthew 5:23-24

So if you are offering your gift at the altar and there remember that your brother has something against you, leave your gift there before the altar and go. First be reconciled to your brother, and then come and offer your gift.

Luke 23: 33-34

And when they came to the place that is called The Skull, there they crucified him, and the criminals, one on his right and one on his left. And Jesus said, "Father, forgive them, for they know not what they do. "And they cast lots to divide his garments.

Hebrews 12:14

Strive for peace with everyone, and for the holiness without which no one will see the Lord.

Prayer:

Dear Father,

I come to You today with a gift! Your Word says when I bring to You a wrong that has been done against me, You count it as a gift. I give to You the person who violated my trust! The one who offended me and was vindictive towards me. This person stole from me. They took something from me that cannot be replaced. They were supposed to love me and support me, but instead, they used me for their own good. But today, my Lord, I make no more judgements against them. I bring this person to Your Throne Room to settle the debt that has been in my soul. I choose to forgive them. The debt that I have had against them is now paid with forgiveness. I bring You my pain, and resentment. I ask You Father to lift this negative emotion from my heart. I repent for holding a grudge and making judgements. Jesus, I don't want to become bitter and I don't want to stay angry. So, now I give it all to YOU! I trust You with the results of my life. I know You are in charge of my life, and I am ok with HOW You are writing my story. I give up my rights to be disappointed, offended and upset. I trust You. I know Your ways are higher than my ways, and Your thoughts are higher than my thoughts. I ask You to align my thoughts with yours! Show me Your ways and help me not to have bad feelings towards my of-fender. I make the exchange in Your *Throne Room* my Lord. I give You this gift of offense and anger and now the results are in Your hands. I choose to forgive, and I choose to walk in forgiveness. I will not pick this back up! Even though my heart may be pulled to go back, today, I declare, I will not turn back in the most powerful name of Jesus! I love You! Amen!

PERSONAL THOUGHTS

Day 10

Cast All Your Cares

__1 Peter 5:6-7__ (NKJV)
Therefore humble yourselves under the mighty hand of
God, that He may exalt you in due time, __casting all your__
__care upon Him, for He cares for you__.

__Psalm 55:22__ (NLV)
__Give all your cares to the Lord and He will give you__
__strength__. He will never let those who are right with Him be
shaken.

__Matthew 11:29-30__ (KJV)
Take my yoke upon you, and learn of me; for I am meek
and lowly in heart: and ye shall find rest unto your souls.
For my yoke is easy, and my burden is light.

Do you know HOW to cast your cares? Do you know what it looks like to cast all your cares upon the Lord?

Look at all three of these texts. You have one from Peter who is giving a prophetic word to the church to cast all ours cares upon the Lord, for He cares for us! Then you have a word from David in the Psalms. Again, he is encouraging us to give every burden, every care to the Lord and He will give you strength. Then, we have a word from Jesus who explains to us HOW to cast our cares.

Where ever you look in scripture, you will see that Jesus is always wanting to make an exchange with us. Have you ever thought about why we call it "scripture"? Look at the root word of scripture. SCRIPT! A script isn't just for reading, but it's for acting out. If you give an actor or actress a role in a movie, you will give them a script to read first, to study and memorize then they will act it out.

It's the same way with us. God has given us the bible, it is our script, to read and study. When we are reading it, we have to put ourselves in the story. Then we walk it out in our everyday life.

Can you walk with me now through the life of Peter? Imagine Peter! What do you think he looks like? What kind of personality do you think he has according to the way he acted in scripture? In my imagination, I see him as a ruddy Jew. I imagine him as a light skinned, maybe blue eyes, very tall, broad shoulders, a manly man, big mouth, hot tempered, an exaggerator of the truth, a fighting man, a drinking man, boastful and prideful. This is my view before Jesus restored Peter. But after he was restored, Peter was a changed man. The way I see him after his restoration is strong, courageous, bold for Jesus, not ashamed, wise, patient, even tempered, strong leader, a powerful man of God, full of faith, full of truth, full of healing power, man on a mission, and a man who sees his future and not his past.

So, when he said, *"humble yourselves under the mighty hand of God, that He may exalt you in due time, **casting all your care upon Him, for He cares for you**."*

I'm not just reading the scripture, but I'm reading the script. Not only am I reading the script, but the scripture is reading me! I can see Peter, but I can see me too! Peter knew what he was talking about. When he said, "humble yourselves" he was asking you to humble yourself or God will humble you. It's less painful if you just humble yourself. He also knew Jesus would perform what He said He would do. Jesus told Peter he would build a church for the kingdom of heaven and not even the gates of hell would prevail against it. So, Peter knew how to cast his cares on the Lord, he knew Jesus loved him, and Jesus would finish what HE started!

What about David? How do you see him? You know all the bible stories! David and Goliath! David and Bathsheba! My heart is all over the place already! This is the way I picture David. He's tall, ruddy, and handsome with big muscles and a harp. In one pocket he has a sling shot and back in his tent he has a sword along with Goliath's head! Not to mention all the foreskins of every Philistine he ever killed (there are just some things I can't imagine). Then I see him with a crown on his head, in a mansion, a little complacent, staring at a beauty woman bathe! Well, the story goes south from there. He gets Bathsheba pregnant and has her husband killed by putting him on the front lines of battle, so he can have his wife and cover up his mess! At the same time, the Bible says he is a man after God's own heart. We all have read the book of Psalms and how powerful it is. We see him swimming in his tears, we see him moaning and groaning to the Lord, we see him praising, dancing and singing, we see him joyful, happy, then sad and mad! David knew what he was talking about when he penned, *"Give all your cares to the Lord and He will give you strength!"*

What about Jesus? Can you take a moment to imagine Him? He was born of a virgin. Mary conceived a child by the Holy Spirit. Can you imagine that? Look at the miracle here? How and why? This is the way I see it by reading the script of the scriptures over and over. God the Father, God the Son, and God the Holy Spirit have always been one, but all three have a distinct role. In the beginning they all three were there. They were there when Adam and Eve were created. They were all three there when Lucifer was thrown out of heaven. I see Jesus all through the Old Testament "hidden," and I see him "revealed" in the New Testament. The way He was revealed was by leaving His place in heaven and becoming 100% man, and 100% Deity! Walking this earth, feeling pain as a human, feeling emotion as 100% man then feeling the pain of death, hell and the grave. I see Him kind, compassionate, loving, caring and merciful. Yet, I see Him bold, honest, smart, intelligent, full of wisdom, full of knowledge, strong, courageous and powerful. I see Him working miracles, fulfilling every prophesy, dying on the cross, raised from the dead and seated at the right hand of the Father in heavenly places interceding for you and me. Try to imagine Jesus. When you read the word, just don't read it as scripture, but read it as a script. Jesus said, "Take my yoke upon you." He is saying His yoke (teachings) is easy and His burden is light. He said that we can learn from HIM.

When you open the eyes of your heart and look at the scripture as alive and powerful, it will change your life. You won't talk the same, you won't think the same, you won't live the same. Everything that Jesus ever touched, He changed! The Word will change your life when you look at it in a different way. Don't read the scripture just to find approval with God and man. But read it with an open heart. The way we open our heart is too SEE the Word and let the Word come alive as we read. Look at this scripture in Hebrews!

> **Hebrews 4:1-12-13 (NLV)**
> *God's Word is living and powerful. It is sharper than a sword that cuts both ways. It cuts straight into where the soul and spirit meet and it divides them. It cuts into the joints and bones. It tells what the heart is thinking about and what it wants to do. No one can hide from God. His eyes see everything we do. We must give an answer to God for what we have done.*

Yes! The Word of God is powerful. It reads me! It can tell the difference between my soul and spirit. It divides! God knows my heart. He knows my motive. He knows how much I can bear. So, saying all that, let's take another look at what Peter said. Peter finally got it. He understood the power of new beginnings, everyday! With Jesus, every day is a new day. He said to cast all my cares upon the Lord, because He cares for me. David said to give all my burdens, my worries to the Lord, for He will make me strong.

What are you worried about? What is bothering you? What is stealing your joy? If you take a moment to imagine what your "burden" looks like, Jesus is ready and waiting to make an exchange with you. Won't you come with me to the *Throne Room* of God and let's make the exchange right now?

Are you believing something about yourself,
your circumstance or God to be the absolute truth,
that really is not true?

- Larry Napier

Prayer:

Dear Abba Father!

I open my heart to You completely today. I ask You to open the eyes of my heart, so I can see You. Show me the truth about myself and about how You feel about me. I ask You to tear down every barrier that gets in my way. Jesus, sometimes life gets so heavy and dark, I need Your light to shine through my darkness. I put on the garment of praise for the spirit of heaviness. I ask You to show me my ways and create in me a clean heart. Renew within me a right spirit. I declare that strongholds are broken over my life. Today I cast all my cares upon You. All my worries! All my concerns! All my doubt! All my disappointment! All my loss! All my negative emotions! I come to Your Throne Room and I make an exchange before You! I exchange my way of thinking to a higher way of thinking. I give You the secret sins of my heart that are hidden from people, but not You. Put in me a brand-new heart! I repent for not trusting You and for blaming You. I took upon myself to worry, to hold grudges or resentment. But now I cast it off me. I throw it off! I don't want it! I want YOU! I want all of You! You said I can TAKE Your yoke for it is easy. Now, I receive it! I receive the anointing of ease! My soul will rest in You O God! My soul will rejoice in You O God! I receive all Your love for me. I receive all Your healing for me. I receive all Your gifts for me. The struggle is real Jesus. But You already know it. You lived it! You will defend me. You will help me. You will never leave me. You will provide for me. Thank You Jesus! Thank you, my Lord, for opening up the heavens, and the door to Your Throne Room so I can meet with You. Your Word says I can go in and out and I will find food! Seal Your Word upon my heart! In Jesus name, Amen.

PERSONAL THOUGHTS

_____

_____

_____

_____

_____

_____

Day 11

The Kind Intentions of God

Jeremiah 31:3-4 (NKJV)
The Lord has appeared of old to me, saying: Yes, I
have loved you with an everlasting love; Therefore with
lovingkindness I have drawn you.
Again I will build you, and you shall be rebuilt, O virgin of
Israel!
You shall again be adorned with your tambourines, And
shall go forth in the dances of those who rejoice.

God absolutely has kind intentions towards you and very positive thought for your life. In **Jeremiah 29:11** He says, "I know the plans I have for you." One translation says, "I know the THOUGHTS I have for you." God is intentional in His plan. He has already equipped you for the journey.

Hebrews 13:20-23 (NLT)
Now may the God of peace—who brought up from the
dead our Lord Jesus,
the great Shepherd of the sheep, and ratified an eternal
covenant with His blood—
*may **HE equip you** with ALL you need. for doing His will.*
*May He **produce in you**,*
*through the power of Jesus Christ, **every good thing** that*
is pleasing to Him.
All glory to Him forever and ever! Amen.

All the gifts you were born with is part of how God has equipped you. He is so loving and kind that He put a gift in each and every one of us. For instance, I have been a singer since I can remember. My mom and dad were both singers. I come from a line of singers in my family. This is one of my gifts! God has a plan for my life. He will use my gift to escort my destiny. The devil will not give you your destiny on a silver platter. But God will! The treasure is inside you! Some of you have a gift of detail. You see things no one else can see. God wants to use that to bring about HIS perfect will in your life. Some of you have the gift of numbers, and math. God wants to use your gift for HIS glory. God has equipped some of you to know how to fix things and create things. God has a plan for you! His intentions for you are good, loving and kind! He wants you to fix what is broken, because that is exactly what HE does! He heals the broken-hearted *(Psalm 147:3)*. He wants you to sing and rejoice over your life, because that is exactly what He is doing over you! *(Zephaniah 3:17)*

The Lord said to Jeremiah, "Hey Jeremiah, I have loved you from the very beginning. From your mother's womb I had already written your story. And now it is my love and my kindness drawing you to ME!" He went on to say to him, "Jeremiah, if anything or anyone tries to tear to you down, don't worry, I will build you back. I will build and rebuild. I will construct and re-construct. I have an everlasting love for you. I am kind to you on purpose. I am intently leaning towards you. I love you!"

When I read this passage, this is exactly how I felt it. God's heart toward you is open and loving and kind. He is not mean! He's good! He wants to show you His glory and His kindness.

Look at what Paul said in the book of Ephesians:

> **Ephesians 2:7** *(NKJV)*
> *that in the ages to come He might show the exceeding riches of His grace in His kindness toward us in Christ Jesus.*

God created you. He knitted you together in your mother's womb. He has not made a mistake about where you were born and to whom you were born. He has a plan! In the middle of evil, God still has a plan, and it is still good! The color of your skin, He calls it good. The color of your hair, He calls it good. The size of your body, He calls it good. The manner of your personality, He calls it good! He has equipped you and make no mention about it, He does not make mistakes! *Psalm 139* says, "you were created perfectly, wonderfully by God!" Whether you are an introvert or extrovert, God did it and He calls it good! What God has called good, don't let anyone call bad or ugly. God is not a man that He would lie or make mistakes! Look at this!

2 Corinthians 12:9-11

But he said to me, "My grace is sufficient for you, for my power is made perfect in weakness." Therefore I will boast all the more gladly about my weaknesses, so that Christ's power may rest on me. That is why, for Christ's sake, I delight in weaknesses, in insults, in hardships, in persecutions, in difficulties. For when I am weak, then I am strong.

Did you see that? Even when you are weak, and in your mistakes, God's power is still at work in you for even in your weakness, you are made strong!

God has promised to take what the devil meant for harm in your life and turn it around for your good. So, you win! God has equipped you! God has kind intentions toward you.

The way you are drawn to God is by love and kindness!

David said it like this:

Psalm 63:3

Because Your loving-kindness is better than life, My lips shall praise You.

Isaiah said it like this:

Isaiah 63:7

I will mention the loving-kindnesses of the Lord and the praises of the Lord,
According to all that the Lord has bestowed on us, And the great goodness toward the house of Israel, which He has bestowed on them according to His mercies,
According to the multitude of His loving-kindnesses.

Paul says it like this:

> **Ephesians 4:32**
> *And be kind to one another, tenderhearted, forgiving one another, even as God in Christ forgave you...*

Then in the book of Titus he sums up what happened to me!

> **Titus 3:4-6** *(NKJV)*
> *But when the **kindness** and the love of God our Savior **toward man** appeared, not by works of righteousness which we have done, but according to His mercy He saved us, through the washing of regeneration and renewing of the Holy Spirit, whom He poured out on us abundantly through Jesus Christ our Savior.*

Let's take a closer look at this:

- Kindness reached out to you to save you
- Love reached out to you to save you
- Kindness and Love is what saves man
- Not by works, nothing you deserved, you can't do anything to earn it, and you can't do anything to take it away
- But all because God has MERCY on YOU and ME

NOW GOD SAYS HE WANTS US TO SHOW THIS SAME KIND OF KINDNESS TO THE WORLD!

REMEMBER? Salvation is the first step! We walk through the DOOR (Jesus) but as we are walking, we are being drawn by the Holy Spirit!

Jesus wants you to encounter His kindness today and His love. It comes from the Throne Room. When you make a habit of entering in to His presence, you will find that Jesus is not angry with You, but He loves you and He wants to change your life. You will find out He is nicest person you ever meet in your whole life. Everything God touches, He changes. When you encounter HIM, you will not leave His presence the same. YOU WILL BE CHANGED!

How does He do it? It is by His Love, His kindness, His compassion on us and His unfailing mercy.

Imagine this with me for a moment. Think of the nicest person you know. Write their name down. Now magnify that by 10,000! That is our Lord Jesus. He is KIND!

Dictionary.com gives us the synonyms of the word KIND; Mild, benign, benignant, gentle, tender, compassionate, kind, gracious, kindhearted.

Kindness implies a sympathetic attitude toward others, and a willingness to do good or give pleasure. Kindness implies a deep-seated characteristic shown by a considerate behavior: Kindhearted implies an emotionally sympathetic nature, *a kind face.*

Jesus is kind, gentle, tender, compassionate, gracious, kindhearted and has a sweet disposition. Even when He convicts us, even when He teaches us! He's just pure love flowing like a fountain with kindness that never runs dry. That is Who He is!

God sent Jesus because of His kind intentions towards us.

> ***Ephesians 1:5** (AMP)*
> *He predestined and lovingly planned for us to be adopted to Himself as [His own] children through Jesus Christ, in accordance with the **kind intention** and good pleasure of His will—*

It says you are chosen. You are hand-picked! All you have to do is say YES to Him and He will adopt you to be His son or daughter through Christ Jesus.

Let's keep reading!

> ***Ephesians 1:6-10** (AMPC)*
> *[So that we might be] to the praise and the commendation of His glorious grace (favor and mercy), which He so freely bestowed on us in the Beloved. In Him we have redemption (deliverance and salvation) through His blood, the remission (forgiveness) of our offenses (shortcomings*

and trespasses), in accordance with the riches and the generosity of His gracious favor, which He lavished upon us in every kind of wisdom and understanding (practical insight and prudence), Making known to us the mystery (secret) of His will (of His plan, of His purpose). [And it is this:] In accordance with His good pleasure (His merciful intention) which He had previously purposed and set forth in Him, [He planned] for the maturity of the times and the climax of the ages to unify all things and head them up and consummate them in Christ, [both] things in heaven and things on the earth.

Did you see that? Can you put yourself in this story? Put your name beside it! There is a story being written and it's a love story between you and Jesus. And He is consummating them in Christ from heaven to earth. From the Throne Room of Grace! How powerful! How loving! How thoughtful! How kind! Jesus is head over hills in love with you. His heart is kind towards you. He wants to reveal mysteries to you. He wants to reveal the secret things of God to you. He wants to reveal Himself to you.

I want to encourage you to get your head free from worry and fear and get your heart set on Jesus. He will show you His love if you open up your heart to Him! This is His kind intention towards you.

Prayer:
Dear Abba Father,
Thank YOU for Your unfailing love, mercy and kindness upon me! Lord, you're Word says with your kindness you will draw me unto yourself. Your Word says, with Your love and kindness, you will build me and I will be rebuilt. Father, I come to You in the most Powerful name of Jesus, asking You to build me, restore the foundation of my life and rebuild what has been torn down. Every area Satan has touched and destroyed in my life, I ask You to build back what he has torn down. My marriage I give to You and ask You to build a strong foundation with love, kindness and respect. I give to You my children and I ask You to build their lives. Surround my children with Your divine protection and may they fill Your loving kindness even as I have felt You. You are touching me even now as I reach out to

You. You are restoring everything the enemy has stolen. Lord, I put You in remembrance (Isaiah 43:26) of Your word and what You have said. Lord, You have said not one word will fall to the ground! I thank You that my latter days will be better than my past. I thank You for You are restoring back to me my health, my finances, my broken relationships, my marriage, my children and my destiny! You are love and You are great. I praise You Lord, for You are worthy to receive all the glory for all the great things You are doing in my life. Now, I ask You, Holy Spirit, to give me the Dunamis power to be kind to every person I meet so I can be the reflection of Jesus. In Jesus name I pray, Amen!

PERSONAL THOUGHTS

Day 12

The Power of Words

> *Mark 11:22-24 (NKJV)*
> *So Jesus answered and said to them, "Have* **faith** *in God. For assuredly, I say to you, whoever* **says** *to this mountain, 'Be removed and be cast into the sea,' and does not* **doubt** *in his heart, but* **believes** *that those things he says will be done, he will have whatever he says. Therefore I say to you, whatever things you* **ask** *when you* **pray**, *believe that you* **receive** *them, and you will have them*

The keys words in this passage are:

- **Faith** in God
- **Says** to the mountain
- No **doubt** in the heart
- **Believes** it will be done
- **Ask** in faith
- **Pray** out loud
- **Receive** what you say

Remember, Jesus is always interested more in relationship with you than anything. He wants you to have a date with Him every day and talk things out with Him. He wants you to have faith in Him, that He hears you and He will respond to you.

Let's look at the power of our words in these passages!

> *Jeremiah 15:9*
> *This is how the LORD responds: "If you return to me, I will restore you so you can continue to serve me. If you __speak good words__ rather than worthless ones, you will be my spokesman. You must influence them; do not let them influence you!*

Psalm 19:14 *(NKJV)*
*Let the words of my mouth and the meditation of my heart
be acceptable in Your sight,*

Psalm 141:3 *(NKJV)*
*Set a guard, O Lord, over my mouth; Keep watch over the
door of my lips.*

Proverbs 12:14 *(NLV)*
*A man will be filled with good from the fruit of his words,
and the work of a man's hands will return to him.*

Proverbs 12:18 *(NLV)*
*There is one whose foolish words cut like a sword, but the
tongue of the wise brings healing.*

Proverbs 15:1 *(NLV)*
*A gentle answer turns away anger, but a sharp word
causes anger.*

As you can tell, the Bible has a lot to say about our words. It goes on and on! But Jesus went a step further with it. He said basically, whatever is in your heart, you will speak, and if you speak it, you will have it. And if it is in your heart, you will dwell on it, think on it, dream of it, imagine it until it is a part of your daily talk and prayer. You will have whatever you say!

So, if you walk around saying things like this:
- Nothing good ever happens to me
- I never win anything
- I'm always sick and tired
- I'm never going to get out of debt
- My kids are rebellious
- I'll never meet the right person
- I'll never be able to buy a house
- My life is a wreck
- I'll never be married
- I'll never have a good job

Then guess what? You will have what you believe! If you believe nothing good ever happens to you, then nothing good will happen to you. Jesus said it! If you confess with your mouth and believe in your heart that you are always sick, and you will never get out of debt, and your kids are rebellious, then you will have those things that you confess and believe. If the words of your mouth speak on negative things, then you will have those negative things. The Bible says a wise person will speak words of life. Every day is new and should be a time of renewing our mind and our hearts. Let me ask you this? Do you ever think about what you think on? Do you ever think before you speak? Do you have the tendency to speak negative words instead of words of life?

Proverbs 15:4 *(ESV)*
A gentle tongue is a tree of life,
but perverseness in it breaks the spirit.

Proverbs 15:28 *(NLT)*
The heart of the godly thinks carefully before speaking.

Proverbs 16:24 *(NIV)*
Gracious words are a honeycomb,
sweet to the soul and healing to the bones.

Proverbs 17:27 *(NASB)*
He who restrains his words has knowledge,
And he who has a cool spirit is a man of understanding.

Proverbs 18:21 *(NIV)*
The tongue has the power of life and death,
and those who love it will eat its fruit.

Proverbs 31:26 *(NLT)*
When she speaks, her words are wise,
and she gives instructions with kindness.

Matthew 12:36 *(NASB)*
But I tell you that every careless word that people speak,
they shall give an accounting for it in the day of judgment.

Matthew 12:37 *(NLT)*
The words you say will either acquit you or condemn you.

Matthew 15:11 *(NLT)*
It's not what goes into your mouth that defiles you; you are defiled by the words that come out of your mouth.

Matthew 15:18 *(NASB)*
But the things that proceed out of the mouth come from the heart, and those defile the man

James 1:26 *(NLT)*
If you claim to be religious but don't control your tongue, you are fooling yourself, and your religion is worthless.

These are some strong truths! Our life will follow our words. Our words follow what is in the heart. And what we really believe is in the heart of a person. So, in essence, your life will follow what you believe!

Let's talk straight a minute. The Bible is a guide for our life. It is a lamp unto our feet. It sheds light where there is darkness. God is light, and God is love. So, light is God and love is God. God spoke the world into existence. When God speaks, things happen. And Jesus is telling us that we have the same power. God said, "let there be light, and there was light." The Word of God tells us if we speak life, then there will be life! Jesus said you will have whatever you SAY!

How many times do our words contradict one another. Speaking out of both sides of our mouth! Have you ever done that before? I certainly have!

James 3:8-12 *(NLV)*
But no man can make his tongue say what he wants it to say. It is sinful and does not rest. It is full of poison that kills. With our tongue we give thanks to our Father in heaven. And with our tongue we speak bad words against men who are made like God. Giving thanks and speaking bad words come from the same mouth. My Christian brothers, this is not right! Does a well of water give good water and bad water from the same place? Can a fig tree give olives or can a grape-vine give figs? A well does not give both good water and bad water.

This is why David said:

Psalm 51:10 *(NLV)*
Make a clean heart in me, O God. Give me a new spirit
that will not be moved.

It all boils down to a heart issue! Every day when we get up, we have to start over, taking every thought into captivity, and bring our thoughts to the Throne Room of God and receive the power of the Holy Spirit to overcome negativity and doubt.

Philippians 4:8 *(NKJV) Meditate on These Things*
Finally, brethren, whatever things are true, whatever things
are noble, whatever things are just, whatever things are
pure, whatever things are lovely, whatever things are of
good report, if there is any virtue and if there is anything
praiseworthy—meditate on these things.

We should meditate on these things. We should imagine these things. We should carry this kind of spirit around with us in our hearts.

Ephesians 3:20 *(NKJV)*
Now to Him who is able to do exceedingly abundantly
above all that we ask or think, according to the power that
works in us,

So, God is saying, if you can think it, see it, imagine it, then I will do it. Not only will I do what you ask, I will go beyond what you ask. I will give you more. I will do even more than your mind can comprehend.

No eye has seen, no mind can imagine what all God has instore for those who love Him.

I want to share a story with you. A story of hope and encouragement. This lady in our church believed what **Matthew 11** said. She did all these things!

- She had **Faith** in God
- She **Spoke** to the mountain of debt

- She did not **doub**t in the heart
- She **Believed** it would be done
- She **Asked** in faith
- She **Prayed** out loud
- She **Receives** what she said

Hi Janet. Here is the story behind my student loan repayment award testimony.

I am a public health professor. That required me to have 3 degrees and about 22 years of formal education. This required me to have student loans which by the end of the 3 degrees totaled about $90K! This is very common for PhDs, physicians, etc… so you just get used to the idea that you will just pay these payments forever. I was paying about $600/month.

A few years ago, I heard about a loan repayment program with the National Institutes of Health. They repay student loans for people who are academics or physicians and are doing research. As you can imagine, this program is EXTREMELY competitive because people really want to shed student loan debt. I started applying for the program back in 2014. Every year, I kept getting rejected or would get to the final round and not get funded. It was very discouraging, but I always called and asked for feedback and improved my application the next year based on the feedback….it seemed to never be enough. This year, I didn't want to apply. I just said forget it… but God sent my mentor to reach out to me. She asked me to let her know when I had my application ready so that she could write my letter of recommendation. I thought… if she is gonna reach out to me and believes in me… then I've got to gather the strength to try again. Her email sparked something inside me… so I decided to put together the absolute best application I could and stand on God's promises. Here's some things I did:

1. I prayed and spent time with God. I tried my best to put God first. I always paid my tithes no matter what and believed God when He said to «try Him» in that area.

2. I persevered and never gave up. Even though I didn't see the promise… I believed it was for me and used the time that was seemingly in the "wilderness" to get better and to improve not only my application, but ME

3. I SAW myself receiving that award. Every time we did the declaration at church I pictured that student loan being gone when Pastor Cary said "debts paid off"… .I would love when he said it twice or more!!

4. I downloaded someone else's award email that they posted on social media. I looked at it every day and pictured my name being there and how I would feel when I saw that email with my name on it.

5. I made my password Loan Repayment Plan Awardee 2018… so that every time I entered the application site, I told myself that I was getting this award

6. In times of adversity, I stood on God's promises. There were times when the loan repayment office emailed me and said some type of documentation was missing or that a document was missing information. My first response was to panic… but I would pull it together and say no Lord, I know this is mine… work it out… and they would email me and say "We're sorry… everything is fine"… .

7. I asked other people to believe and pray with me!

8. I finally woke up one morning and read my email that said, "Congratulations you have received the award… " and I rejoiced, shouted, cried and gave God glory because now the promise was manifested. It came to pass!

9. Now, I have to care for the promise and give my best self to the research I said I would do in my application so that my work pleases God and makes a difference in the lives of people with sickle cell disease.

What happened here? I can tell you what happened! The Word of God came alive in her heart, she spoke it, she believed it, she did not give up on it, she worked for it, she asked God for it, she had faith in God that He would bring it to pass!

> **Mark 11:22-24** *(NKJV)*
> *So Jesus answered and said to them, "Have* **faith** *in God.*
> *For assuredly, I say to you, whoever* **says** *to this mountain,*
> *'Be removed and be cast into the sea,' and does not*

doubt *in his heart, but* **believes** *that those things he says will be done, he will have whatever he says. Therefore, I say to you, whatever things you* **ask** *when you* **pray**, *believe that you* **receive** *them, and you will have them*

Prayer:

Dear Jesus,

I come before you today with an open heart. I ask You to create in me a clean heart that is pure and acceptable in your sight. Father, I come to Your Throne Room of Grace and ask for You to forgive me and wash away from my heart every negative thought! Every doubtful thought! Help me oh Lord to think, meditate, imagine the promise coming to pass. I don't want to be double minded and to speak out of both sides of my mouth. I choose today to believe You for the promise. Your Word says You watch over Your Word very carefully and You will perform it. You will not let one thing fall to the ground. So today I speak life and blessings over my life, over my marriage, over my finances, over my health, and over my destiny. I declare and believe in my heart that all my debts are paid off. I declare and believe my body will line up with Your word and I am healed. I declare and believe will not hold any grudges or unforgiveness in my heart. I come to Your Throne Room of Grace and lay down at Your feet all my pain, my frustration, doubt, worry, fear, concerns about the future! I believe You love me, and You are working on my behalf. I believe You hear me when I pray! I believe Your word Father. You said if I can imagine it, You can perform it! I know You are working all things together for my good. I trust You. I believe in miracles. I believe You can do anything. Your Words says through YOU, I can do anything. I pray Father, You will increase me, bless me, enlarge my territory, bless my family, make me whole in spirit, soul and body, touch my business, touch my bank account, touch my mind, give me ideas from Your Throne Room. Help me to see through Your eyes and not through my own. Jesus, I know You are interceding for me that my Faith will not fail me! I believe I have the things that I am asking for. I believe Father! I can see it! I hold it in my heart! I thank You Father, for there is a miracle in the making for me today! You are working behind the scenes. You have not forgotten me, and I have not forgotten Your promises! I love You so much Lord! Thank you for all you have done for me and for all You are going to do in my future! I make a bold declaration from the top of my lungs, I TRUST YOU! WILL NOT DOUBT, I WILL NOT FEAR! In the most powerful name of Jesus I pray, Amen!

PERSONAL THOUGHTS

Day 13

Choose Life

Deuteronomy 30:15-19 (NKJV)
"See, I have set before you today life and good, death
and evil, in that I command you today to love the
Lord your God, to walk in His ways, and to keep His
commandments, His statutes, and His judgments, that
you may live and multiply; and the Lord your God will
bless you in the land which you go to possess. But if your
heart turns away so that you do not hear, and are drawn
away, and worship other gods and serve them, I announce
to you today that you shall surely perish; you shall not
prolong your days in the land which you cross over the
Jordan to go in and possess. I call heaven and earth as
witnesses today against you, that I have set before you life
and death, blessing and cursing; therefore choose life, that
both you and your descendants may live;

I have a lot of people who come to my office to talk about the pain in their heart. They tell me stories of their life and the anguish and turmoil they are in because of the decisions they made while they were in their 20's. Yes! The decisions you make now can affect the rest of your life. This is why we should be taught early on to make good decisions.

In our 20's or approaching 20's are very vital, crucial years. These are the years you will make the most important decisions of your life. You will decide which career path to take. Which school to go to in order to get the career you want. You will choose your spouse. You will choose how many kids you want to have. You will choose your dwelling place etc. Many times, the freedom of becoming an adult can be overwhelming. After all, daddy's not looking, and mom doesn't know what you're up to. There is a tendency to go wild! You're still trying to figure out how to use this freedom. One drink leads to another. A "one-night stand" leads to another "one-night stand." One mistake after the other leads to the next mistake. But the truth is, with freedom comes responsibility. With responsibility comes making good choices. With making good choices comes someone who still has some guidance. The book of Psalms says it like this:

> **Psalm 119:105** *(NLV)*
> *Your Word is a lamp to my feet and a light to my path.*

The Word will guide you in darkness and confusion.

> **Job 10:12** *(NKJV)*
> *You have granted me life and favor, and Your care has preserved my spirit.*

The Word will grant you **LIFE**, if you choose it

> **Psalm 16:11** *(NKJV)*
> *You will show me the path of life; In Your presence is fullness of joy; At Your right hand are pleasures forevermore.*

There are consequences to the decisions we make. Everything you do in life is because of a decision you have made. Believe it or not, but you choose to be happy or to be bitter. You choose to forgive or not to forgive. You choose to be positive or to be negative. You choose to read your bible or to not read your bible. You choose to tell the truth or to lie. You choose to commit adultery or fornication. You choose whether or not you are going to look at pornography. You choose whether or not you are going to church. Every day you are making decisions that will either bring LIFE to you, or death to you.

> **Galatians 6:7-9** *(NKJV)*
> *Do not be deceived, God is not mocked; for whatever a man sows, that he will also reap. For he who sows to his flesh will of the flesh reap corruption, but he who sows to the Spirit will of the Spirit reap everlasting life. And let us not grow weary while doing good, for in due season we shall reap if we do not lose heart.*

Your decisions will affect you greatly. When you are in your college years there is so much opportunity to make bad decisions. Some of you have so much baggage already going into your twenties. But you have to be careful because you will reap what you sow.

For me, by the time I had graduated from high school, I had already attended 11 different schools, moved from city to city and state to state, been through foster care, been through sexual abuse, been through abandonment, just to arrive at the age of 17 at a place called "The Statesboro Church of God." The evangelist on that cold Sunday night in January gave an altar call to those who were tired of the life they were living, weary from the world of sin, to the one who was thirsty for something more, hurting from the pain of their past and lost in a world of sin. He gave way for me to give my heart to Jesus and make Him Lord and Savior of my life. I felt the Holy Spirit pulling on the strings of my heart to go to the altar. I had a decision to make. Will I walk away from my old life and leave it behind, or will I embrace a new season in my life and make a change? Well, my friend, in the month of January 1988, my senior year in high school, I ran to the altar with tears streaming down my face and gave my heart completely to Jesus. I was weeping and singing in the altar. I felt the Holy Spirit sweep over me and wash me clean and He put so much love and joy in my heart. I felt as if He put a new heart within me.

The best decision I ever made in my life was making Jesus Christ my Lord and Savior. He changed everything. He touched me, He cleansed me, He turned my life around. I was wounded, I was broken, I was abandoned and forsaken and He took me in and gave me a brand-new identity. My life has been built on that one decision I made at the age of 17. Through that decision, I met my husband, found my calling, found my career and now at the age of 48 I have seen God build my life off of my brokenness.

I want to tell you one more story about a beautiful woman in her college years who was a devout Christian who made a decision that haunted her for many years afterwards until she came into my office at the age of 50 to find healing for her soul.

I had known this lady for many years. She was tall and slender with cheek bones carved to the highest of perfection. Her eyebrows set the tone for her overall beauty. Her skinned glowed like a diamond reflected in the sun. Her dark, silky hair fell into a swinging inverted bob. Her smile and inward beauty exceeded her outward beauty. She was always so kind, generous, sweet, and graceful. She moved with so much grace and balance. Little did I know this lady was dying on the inside. She was hurting so deep and her soul was crying out for help. The more we got to know each other, the more she began to open up to me and tell me about her story.

I will never forget the day she came into my office with her head hung low. She sat down in my chair and she said she had something very shameful to tell me. With tears streaming down her face and the all pain I could see in her chocolate eyes, she confessed about a decision she had made in her twenties. As she walked in the room, I could feel the pain. Immediately my heart began to sink. I was wondering what in the world happened! I could clearly see her soul was in anguish and pain. She had a secret she had never told anyone. She had been carrying it around for all these years.

Finally, she gathered all the strength she had to tell me her secret. The tears that streamed down her face was accompanied by groans and moans that pierced my soul as I heard her gasp for air in between breaths low from the depths of her lungs.

I laid my hands upon her shoulders as she attempted to tell me what happened to try to bring comfort to her. I could feel her grief, her pain, her regret. At the same time, I felt Jesus walk in the room. She began to confess to me that her boyfriend, who later on became her husband, got her pregnant. He was in law school and she was in college and they both could not see any other way out but to get an abortion. They could not wrap their minds around having a baby in all the stress of school. So, they both agreed to get the abortion. He was right there by her side as the doctor walked in the room and began the procedure. She felt guilt grip her soul, but could not say no. She felt darkness come over her and pain as she made a decision that led to death. After the procedure was complete, she bled profusely. He took her home as she laid in bed and cried and cried and bled and bled. On that day, more was taken from her besides the abortion. Her peace of mind was taken. A piece of her soul was ripped from her as they performed the procedure.

Now, here she is in her 50's. Her marriage finally led to divorce from infidelity. After 25 years of marriage and two kids later, she is now guilt ridden that she deserved it all because of the decision she had made. She blamed herself for the divorce and the infidelity of her husband because of what she had done.

That day in my office, I felt Jesus walk in as she poured her heart out to me. I led her to the throne room of God to find healing for her soul. I, too had tears streaming down my face. Not because I was sad, but because I felt HOPE for her. I knew what Jesus could do for her. I showed her the door in heaven that was OPEN for her. She and I walked through that door, (with our imagination), and we walked down the aisle together to meet with Jesus in His Throne Room as a bride would meet her betrothed. The presence of God was electrifying! At the same time, there was love that washed over us like a wave from the ocean washing away guilt and shame. The RESTORER took her hand as she gave HIM all her pain, regret, guilt, and shame. There was a powerful exchange that took place that day as my friend received forgiveness from the Father. She was able to receive forgiveness as she made the exchange, and she was able to forgive herself. No longer would guilt have dominion over her life.

The Lord showed her, as we walked through the healing process together, the "accuser of the brethren," Satan, *(Rev. 12)* had come down with wrath to destroy her through guilt. He was there that day in her twenties influencing her to make a decision because she saw no other way out. Satan is the one to blame. He was convincing in his speech.

He will show you with your imagination, there is no other way. Satan uses your imagination to torture you! So why not use your imagination with God. Go UP to receive wisdom, go UP to receive healing, go UP to receive restoration, go UP to receive forgiveness.

A week after she came in my office, the Lord showed me what to do to bring an end to this chapter of her life. As I walked through Hobby Lobby, I asked the Holy Spirit to show me what He wanted me to do. I just walked around until I heard Him say STOP! I walked by a little treasure chest and He said, "Pick it up and buy it. I will show you what to do." So, I picked it up and put it in my buggy. I walked by the aisle that had pearls. He said to me, "Buy those pearls and a bag to put them in." I bought the beautiful small bag. Then He said to me, "Buy her a pearl necklace with one single pearl." So, I bought a pearl necklace with one single pearl. I took them home and I prayed and asked the Father what He wanted me to do. He led me to my jewelry box to a set of pearl earring I had. He said to me, "Give her those pearl earrings as an offering to ME." With joy I lifted the earrings out as I listened carefully to what He said to do next.

He said to me, "My daughter, I want you to hold a ceremony for her baby. It will be like a funeral and it will bring closure to this chapter of her life. I want you to put one pearl in the treasure box to signify her baby is a treasure and her baby is with Me and she will see her baby again in heaven.

The one single pearl necklace signifies the one child that is not with her now, however she carries the baby in her heart with joy and hope of seeing her again. The pearl earrings signify my love for her as her One and True Love. It says to her she is MY treasure and I am committed to her. I will not leave her, I will not walk away, I will not abandon her. I will be her Husband. I will be her Protector. I will be her Provider. Her baby girl is with Me. Tell her the price has been paid for her redemption. My daughter, when you do this, I will sweep over her and wash her of all the residue that was left behind and erase the pain of her past. I will now build upon her brokenness."

I did exactly what the Lord told me to do. And HE did exactly what He said He would do. The Holy Spirit came upon her, He cleansed her, and He made the final blow to Satan's head! Because Satan is under His feet! And now, Satan is under HER feet as well.

What are you carrying around? Are you carrying guilt of your past? Are you carrying pain from your past? Have you made decisions in your life that has led to torment? Well, it's not too late. Today is your day to make the exchange, just like my friend did. You can do it now. First of all, choose JESUS! He is the best decision you will ever make in your life. Everything will flow out of that powerful decision. Don't hesitate any longer. There is forgiveness for your soul. There is a place for you in the Throne Room of God, right beside Jesus. Since He is alive and well, seated in heavenly places, He said you too can be seated in heavenly places and you too can be ALIVE and WELL.

Prayer:

Dear Abba Father,

What a loving Father You are! You are good, and Your mercy endures FOREVER. Lord, I choose YOU. I choose Life! For You are my life.

Lord, Your word says there is **NOTHING** that can separate us from Your love. When You sent Your Son Jesus, He willingly came down as a man to live and die as a man and to make the sacrifice that would open up the door in heaven, so we could all enter in. You bore our pain! You bore our abandonment! You bore abortion! You bore death itself! You bore murder! You bore abuse! You bore incest! You bore rape! You bore lies, shame, envy, guilt and every other negative emotion that Satan has tried to condemn us with.

Then You (Jesus) took it to the throne room, You took the blood before the Father and there you made propitiation. Right then and there you crushed the head of Satan, you ripped the veil, all of heaven went silent for thirty minutes as your blood sealed the deal! There, it was FINISHED! Thank you, Jesus! Thank you, Father! Lord, You are worthy of all the praise and glory. Who can forgive sins? Who can wipe away a past? Who can heal a broken heart? Who can build on brokenness? Who can give a new beginning? Who can restore? Who can redeem? Who can restore **ALL** the devil has stolen away? No one can but YOU Lord! No one! Only YOU!!! Hallelujah! You are a Redeemer of the breech. You restore the lost. You put us in right standing with You. You made us righteous. No more guilt! No more shame! Lord, I thank You for filling my life with joy, and freedom in the Holy Spirit. I choose YOU. I choose LIFE! I am filled with wisdom. I will continue to make good decision in my life. Now, I come boldly to Your Throne of Grace! This is who I am! I am righteous, because You made me righteous through Your blood and resurrection! Praise be to the Lamb of God!, Who was and is to come! To God Be the Glory! Amen!

PERSONAL THOUGHTS

I Shall Not Want

Psalm 23:1 *(NKJV)*
*The Lord is my shepherd; **I shall not want**.*

The **23rd Psalm** is one of the most famous scriptures in the bible. Most people can quote this scripture. You will hear people read the 23rd Psalm at weddings and funerals. Imagine that! The **23rd Psalm** is one of the most powerful scriptures that people can run to in order to find comfort, peace and encouragement.

There is so much meat in this scripture when you and I could feed off this single Psalm for several weeks. But right now, I want to focus on Verse 1. Every word that is written in **Psalm 23** is based off verse 1. "The Lord is my Shepherd, I shall not want." First of all, it begins with a declaration of whom he belonged to. David made a bold statement to everyone he was around. People knew that Jehovah God was his Shepherd.

What does it mean to have a shepherd? David certainly knew what it was like to BE a shepherd, because he was a little shepherd boy.

Here are some attributes to a Shepherd:

A shepherd faces the ongoing challenge of <u>**teaching**</u> the sheep and goats to obey his commands. Even so, a good shepherd <u>**takes tender care**</u> of the animals in his charge, even <u>**giving them names to which they would respond**</u>.—*John 10:14,16*.

In Spring, each day a shepherd might <u>**lead his flock**</u> from a pen near his home to graze on the fresh, succulent growth in the nearby village pastures. During this season, the birth of lambs and kids would expand the size of the flock. At that time, workers would also shear the winter fleece from the sheep, this was an occasion to celebrate!

After the fields near the village were harvested, the shepherd would allow his sheep to graze on new shoots and on grain left among the stubble. When summer heat set in, **shepherds moved their flocks** to cooler pastures **on higher ground.** For days on end, **shepherds would work** and sleep outdoors, allowing the flock to graze on the steep green slopes and spending the nights guarding the open sheepfolds. At times, the **shepherd would shelter his flock** overnight in a cave, where they would be **protected** from jackals and hyenas. If the howl of a hyena panicked the flock of sheep in the dark of night, **the shepherd's calm reassuring voice would still them.**

Each evening, the **shepherd counted the sheep** and **checked the health** of the animals. In the morning, **he would call,** and the **flock would follow him** to the pasture ground. *(John 10:3,4)* At midday, **shepherds led** the animals to cool pools of water to drink. When the pools dried up, the **shepherd guided** them to a well and drew water for them.

Toward the end of the dry season, a shepherd might move his flock to the coastal plains and valleys. When the cold rains began, he would **lead them back home** to winter indoors. Otherwise, the animals could perish outside in the lashing rains, hailstorms, and snow.

The nucleus of the first line of the *23rd Psalm*, "The Lord is my Shepherd," is saying so much more than "He's my shepherd."

Let's take a deeper look into the nucleus of what the word was really saying by inserting the areas that are bold and underlined above.

- The Lord is my Shepherd, I shall not want
- The Lord is my TEACHER, He takes good CARE of me, I lack nothing
- The Lord knows my name, and I know His voice and I will respond to Him
- The Lord leads me, He is enough
- The Lord moves me to higher ground, I need nothing else
- The Lord is my Shelter, I don't have to beg
- The Lord is my Protector, I have no other needs
- The Lord is my Calm Assurance (His Voice calms me), He's all I need

- The Lord checks in on me and I am counted among Him, I am full
- The Lord looks out for my well- being and my health, He's all I need
- The Lord is calling me, I have no lack
- I will follow the Lord, I have no lack
- The Lord is my guide, I have no lack

The Lord is my Shepherd, therefore I have no lack! This is what David was saying in the first line of this Psalm.

> Believe from a place of abundance rather than lack!
> **- Janet Swanson**

One day I was watching my youngest son play basketball. He was in a tournament in the summer league of high school and AAU. By all means, I am no professional coach for basketball or scout, but I do have discernment, insight and common sense. As I watched them play, I saw something as the Lord was pointing out to me. The Lord spoke to my heart and said, "Look at the other team and focus on their confidence and see 'where' they are playing from." I responded to Him by saying, "What do you mean, Lord?"

He said, "The reason why the other team is winning in not because they are better, but it's because they are playing from a place of abundance, confidence and heart. Therefore, the scoreboard is the evidence of what is happening in the heart and mind of the team. But when you play from a place of 'lack', it is believing you can't do it because of a few mistakes that were made, and you can't find your grip again. When you play from a place of lack, it will lead to a place of defeat in the heart before the game is even over. Victory has to be seen in the heart first before it can be seen on the scoreboard. When you play from a place of abundance instead of lack and no matter what or whom you face, you will end up with the Victory."

It is the same way in life. Sometimes we give up too soon because of the mistakes we have made, and we don't want to get up and start all over again. Until you find that 'place' of abundance to live from, you will automatically fall into default nature that will lead you to a mentality of lack.

In the game of basketball, there is a coach, (shepherd), he's the leader and encourager. He's taking good care of the team. Then you have the assistant coach (another shepherd) who helps the head coach and is always looking out for the team. Then you have the team mates who look to the point guard (another shepherd) who is looking, watching, choosing and strategizing the play to get the ball to the right person who can make some points.

Imagine if you could live your life based on what your future looked like instead of what your past has offered you! All the past will do is keep you stagnant, right there in it. But if that is all you ever dwell on, your past will soon become your present, your future and your destiny. You will keep repeating your past, the same failures, the same traps of the enemy. **This is a mentality of lack**. But as a child of God, the Word says we have been made more than conquerors. When you play from a place of abundance, you have declared with your heart the possibility of what each game holds! A slam dunk! A Steal! A basket whooooshhhhh!

When you learn how to play with the heart, dream with the heart, see with the heart, you will be able to say like David, "The Lord is my Shepherd, I shall not want." It becomes your identity. It becomes your core belief.

He said, "Since the Lord is my Shepherd, I have no lack in my life. I have no need of anything because He (the Good Shepherd) is looking out for me. His eyes are upon me. He is guiding me and protecting me."

It's not to say I don't need people, or I don't need money, or I don't need love. God knows that we have to have money in order to live, and He created us and wired us for love, and God did not create us an "Island" to be alone, by ourselves with no friends at all. No! That is not what David was saying. He was saying at the very core of his being, the Lord God was his everything. He was All in All. He is God of the heavens and earth and everything in it. Bottom line, David trusted God.

Let's take a look at the rest of the Psalm now that we have a better understanding of the attributes of a Shepherd.

The Lord the Shepherd of His People

Psalm 23 *(NKJV)*
A Psalm of David.

*The Lord **is** my shepherd; (King, my Leader)*
I shall not want (I have no lack)
He makes me to lie down (rest) in green pastures; (a place of abundance)
He leads me beside the still waters (He give me peace).
He restores my soul; (He heals my wounded soul, He replenishes my soul)
He leads me in the paths of righteousness (He directs my path in right standing)
For His name's sake. (because I carry HIS name)

Yea, though I walk through the valley (a low place) of the shadow of death, (freezing darkness)
I will fear no evil; (I am not afraid of the darkness)
*For You **are** with me; (by my side)*
Your rod (God's loving discipline) and Your staff (God's Authority), they comfort me.

You prepare a table (you set the table, buy the groceries, cook the meal) before me (for me) in the presence of my enemies; (boldly in the face of my enemy) You anoint my head with oil; (I am filled with the Holy Spirit)
My cup runs over. (My spirit, soul, body and life is overflowing with more than enough)
Surely goodness and mercy shall follow me (goodness and mercy will always have my back)
All the days of my life; (until I take my last breath)
And I will dwell in the house of the Lord (and even when I take my last breath, I will still dwell with HIM forever)
Forever.

God never said we wouldn't walk through valleys, but He did Promise to walk with us through the valley.

God never said we wouldn't fear, but He did say we would not fear the evil.

God never said you wouldn't have an enemy, but He did say He will boldly bless you in the presence of your enemy.

God never said you would never experience darkness, but He did say He will walk with you in the darkness.

Remember this, it was in the valley that God restored his soul! Don't despise the valley experiences in your life. The Word says Jesus is the Lily of the Valley. It is in the valley we will find our life and lose it at the same time.

If you are walking in a valley, know that it is a place of abundance, even in the valley, there is no lack, His presence is with you.

Prayer:
Dear Lord,
I thank You Father for being my Shepherd. You are taking good care of me. You walk before me, You clear the paths for me, You prepare a table for me, and You bless me. You are protecting me, leading me, guiding me every step of the way. Help me Father to see that even though I walk through Valleys, I am walking in abundance, I have no lack. Your word says you will withhold no good thing from me. Thank you, Lord, for fighting battles for me, for looking out for my well-being. Help me to play, live, think from a place of abundance, (no lack), so I can walk in the fullness you have for me. Thank you, my Lord, for your perfect love that cast all fear away. I am filled with Your sweet love. I am filled with Your anointing. You fill up my life until I overflow! Lord, You are more than enough for me. You are my defender. You take up for me, You stand up for me, and You block the attacks of the enemy. I make a bold declaration of Your Word that says YOU RESTORE! Thank You for restoring my soul, restoring my life, restoring my family, restoring my finances, restoring my health, restoring my dreams, and restoring my hope. My hope is in You. I love You and I cherish Your Word and I cherish Your presence. In Jesus name I pray, Amen.

PERSONAL THOUGHTS

Day 15

Running With the Horses

Jeremiah 12:5 (ESV)
If you have raced with men on foot,
and they have wearied you,
how will you compete with horses?
And if in a safe land you are so trusting,
what will you do in the thicket of the Jordan?

Having you ever heard this scripture before? How to run with horses or contend with horses? Before we can understand this scripture, it is important to know what horses can do.

How fast can a horse run? The fastest recorded history of a race horse was recorded at 55 mph. The gallop average is 30 mph.

There are 4 main ways in which a horse can move; these are called walking, trotting, cantering, and galloping.

Horses have a rhythm. Let's look at their rhythm to get a better understanding of this scripture.

The "walk" is a comfortable 4 beat gait.

The "Trot" is an uncomfortable 2 beat gait.

The "Canter/lope" is a 3 beat gait which is asymmetrical and can be fun and unnerving to beginning riders.

The "gallop" is a 4 beat gate, which is asymmetrical high speed that can be thrilling for the rider and during the suspension phase when all feet are off the ground it feels like you're flying.

Have you ever ridden a horse before? It is true, you have to find their rhythm in order to ride one properly. As a rider there is an upbeat and a downbeat, there is an asymmetrical beat for as a musician I would say it is a 3/4 timing. In music you would say 3/4 timing is four measures with 3 beats in each measure.

Running with the horses means more than just wearing yourself out. It is finding the rhythm and adjusting to the pace and timing of the horse. I don't know about you, but when I ride a horse, it can be very scary. I remember the time I was in an open field and I had a friend who was with me and was teaching me how to ride the horse. All of the sudden the horse took off on a gallop and I lost the rhythm fast and the horse beat me so bad. My behind was bruised and so sore, I could barely walk for several days.

Have you ever seen a person who has attempted to ride a horse for the first time? Have you seen how they walk when they get off the horse? It is very comical.

There is a rhythm to catch when you are riding. Here's the catch! If I am going to run with the horses, I have got to understand the rhythm, so I can run. I am not just riding a horse, I am running with the horses.

God was responding to Jeremiah's complaint in **Jeremiah 12:5**, but look at what Jeremiah was complaining about in verses 1-4.

> ### Jeremiah 12:1-4
> *You are right, O God, and you set things right. I can't argue with that. But I do have some questions: Why do bad people have it so good? Why do con artists make it big? You planted them and they put down roots. They flourished and produced fruit. They talk as if they're old friends with you, but they couldn't care less about you. Meanwhile, you know me inside and out. You don't let me get by with a thing! Make them pay for the way they live, pay with their lives, like sheep marked for slaughter. How long do we have to put up with this—the country depressed, the farms in ruin—*
> *And all because of wickedness, these wicked lives? Even*

animals and birds are dying off Because they'll have
nothing to do with God and think God has nothing to do
with them.

Can you hear the weariness in his voice? Can you hear his frustration? I certainly can! You know why? Because I have said this same thing to God.

I was in my 20's and wanted to have a baby so bad, and I tried and tried. Then I saw teenagers in the church getting pregnant, not serving God, and prospering in the one thing that my heart desired. I said to God, "Lord, you know me, You know I love You. You know my heart. Your word has promised me a baby, and I have served you, loved you, followed you and Your blessings are upon them and not me!"

I was running with men, with man's perspective. I had an earthly complaint. I had an earthly prospective. I had an earthly view. At the same time, I trusted God even though I didn't understand. I kept serving Him, even though I suffered emotionally. Now, skip forward 20 years and three handsome boys later, I found out that God had a plan for me the whole time. He was teaching me how to pray, how to see in the spirit, how to trust HIM when life didn't make sense and to believe beyond what I could see.

The Lord responded to Jeremiah's complaint. Notice how God isn't angry with Jeremiah, but He speaks a word in this young man's heart because He knows the future plans He has for him. The Lord said to Jeremiah, "Look my son, how can you prophesy to the nations when you can't even deal with your own community?"

When you have a "Throne Room View," you are looking through the lenses of heaven (the supernatural) and the possibility of success each day holds. When you have an earthly prospective, you are looking through the lenses of the flesh (the natural) and the possibility of failure.

Here is a prophet in the bible who knew how to "run with the horses."

I Kings 18:1-39 (MSG) *(paraphrased by Janet Swanson)*
A long time passed. Then God's word came to Elijah. The
drought was now in its third year. God said to Elijah: "Go

and present yourself to Ahab; I'm about to make it rain on the country." Elijah set out to present himself to Ahab. The drought in Samaria at the time was most severe.

In the middle of the drought, Elijah challenges Ahab and all his false prophets and their gods to a face-off! He said, "You pray to your god for fire to fall from heaven upon this altar and I will pray to my God and whoever answers is the true living God! The key was, they could not light the fire, their god had to do it.

Elijah told the Baal prophets, "Choose your ox and prepare it. You go first, you're the majority. Then pray to your god, but don't light the fire."

So, they took the ox he had given them, prepared it for the altar, then prayed to Baal. They prayed all morning long, "O Baal, answer us!" But nothing happened—not so much as a whisper of breeze. Desperate, they jumped and stomped on the altar they had made.

By noon, Elijah had started making fun of them, taunting, "Call a little louder—he is a god, after all. Maybe he's off meditating somewhere or other, or maybe he's gotten involved in a project, or maybe he's on vacation. You don't suppose he's overslept, do you, and needs to be waked up?" They prayed louder and louder, cutting themselves with swords and knives—a ritual common to them—until they were covered with blood. This went on until well past noon. They used every religious trick and strategy they knew to make something happen on the altar, but nothing happened—not so much as a whisper, not a flicker of response.

Then Elijah told the people, "Enough of that—it's my turn. Gather around." And they gathered. He then put the altar back together for by now it was in ruins. Elijah took twelve stones, one for each of the tribes of Jacob, the same Jacob to whom God had said, "From now on your name is Israel." He built the stones into the altar in honor of

God. Then Elijah dug a fairly wide trench around the altar. He laid firewood on the altar, cut up the ox, put it on the wood, and said, "Fill four buckets with water and drench both the ox and the firewood." Then he said, "Do it again," and they did it. Then he said, "Do it a third time," and they did it a third time. The altar was drenched and the trench was filled with water.

When it was time for the sacrifice to be offered, Elijah the prophet came up and prayed, "O God, God of Abraham, Isaac, and Israel, make it known right now that You are God in Israel, I am your servant, and I'm doing what I'm doing under your orders. Answer me, God; O answer me and reveal to this people that you are God, the true God, and that you are giving these people another chance at repentance."

Immediately the fire of God fell and burned up the offering, the wood, the stones, the dirt, and even the water in the trench.

All the people saw it happen and fell on their faces in awe and worshipped, exclaiming, "God is the true God! God is the true God!"

Now, let's take a deeper look to see how Elijah was running with the horses!

1 Kings 18:41-46 *(MSG)*

Elijah said to Ahab, "Up on your feet! Eat and drink— celebrate! Rain is on the way; I hear it coming."

Ahab did it: got up and ate and drank. Meanwhile, Elijah climbed to the top of Carmel, bowed deeply in prayer, his face between his knees. Then he said to his young servant, "On your feet now! Look toward the sea."

He went, looked, and reported back, "I don't see a thing."

"Keep looking," said Elijah, "seven times if necessary."

And sure enough, the seventh time he said, "Oh yes, a cloud! But very small, no bigger than someone's hand, rising out of the sea."

"Quickly then, on your way. Tell Ahab, 'Saddle up and get down from the mountain before the rain stops you.'" Things happened fast. The sky grew black with wind-driven clouds, and then a huge cloudburst of rain, with Ahab hightailing it in his chariot for Jezreel. **And God strengthened Elijah mightily**. *Pulling up his robe and tying it around his waist,* **Elijah ran** *in front of Ahab's chariot until they reached Jezreel.*

Not only was Elijah running with the horses, he OUTRAN the horses! Imagine that! I can see it right now as the hand of God reached down from "heaven to earth" and gave him all the strength he needed to RUN!

Elijah prayed for rain, and then he heard the sound of rain. Then he waited, anticipated, looked for and expected rain! And guess what? IT RAINED! When he saw the rain, he did a rain-dance-run!

Elijah was running with the horses. And God wants you to run with the horses too! Isaiah says it so well as he heard from heaven and penned these most famous words!

> **Isaiah 40:31** *(ESV)*
> *But they who wait for the Lord shall renew their strength; they shall mount up with wings like eagles; they* ***shall run and not be weary; they shall walk and not faint***.

You have but one life to live. God wants you to live from "heaven to earth" and not from "earth to heaven."

The older we get; the faster time catches up with us. Let's not waste any more time. Let's run this race that is set before us, and let's run with the horses!

You may ask, "How can I run?" Have you ever been to a track meet? Observe what they are wearing. Hardly nothing at all. The men wear a skinny pair of shorts and light weight shoes.

That's what we have to do. We have to get rid of everything that is hindering our walk with the Lord and stopping our gallop in life. Get back in rhythm with God and RUN!!!

Hebrews 12:1-3 (NKJV)
Therefore we also, since we are surrounded by so great
a cloud of witnesses, let us lay aside every weight, and
*the sin which so easily ensnares us, and **let us run** with*
*endurance **the race that is set before** us, looking unto*
***Jesus**, the **author** and **finisher of our faith**, who for the*
joy that was set before Him endured the cross, despising
the shame, and has sat down at the right hand of the
throne of God. For consider Him who endured such
hostility from sinners against Himself, lest you become
weary and discouraged in your souls.

Do you want to run with the horses? If so, make Jesus Christ your Lord and Savior and look to Him for He is the Author of your life. He is writing your beautiful story. He has been there through the dry places of life. He has been there through every storm. He has been there when you felt like you couldn't make it another day, just to find yourself waking up to another horizon. All the dark days of your life is doing nothing but highlighting the shadow of your mountain top experiences and it causes a 3-D effect! He puts the breath in your lungs to sustain you all the days of your life. God has great plans for you! When you catch the wave of His hypnotic rhythm, you will find yourself living from "heaven to earth" doing things that you know you couldn't do without His divine strength and help! You will run with the horses, you will trample over serpents, you will fly and soar like an eagle, you will endure hardship with joy, and finally, you will finish this race STRONG!

Prayer:
Dear Abba Father,
I come to You in the most precious name of Jesus. Today I pour my heart out to You. Teach me to see from "heaven to earth." Teach me to live my life from "heaven to earth." Teach me to pray from "heaven to earth." Teach me to worship from "heaven to earth." I give my whole life to you. I give my pain to you, my past to you, my failures to you, my thoughts to you, my will to you, my family to you, my wealth to you, my lack to you, for in YOU, I am full and not empty.

I throw off everything that will hinder my walk and stop my race. Lord, I pray to catch the wave of Your divine rhythm because I know You are for me. I know You are not against me. I know You love me. I accept all your love, kindness and strength. I declare from this day forward, that I will run with the horses, I will soar with the eagles, I will not be discouraged, I will not quit, but I will finish strong! Because Your powerful Spirit lives within me, I know all things are possible. Teach me to see the possibilities of each day instead of the struggles of each day. Teach me to operate from a place of abundance and not lack.

I ask You Father to restore to me everything the devil has stolen from me. He has stolen from me 'time." Your Word says You will redeem the time!

He has robbed me of my joy! Your Word says there is fullness of joy in Your presence.

He has stolen from me "health." Your Word says that You will bring healing to my body rapidly.

He has stolen my finances. Your Word says since I pay my tithe and offerings, you will open the windows of heaven and pour out a blessing to me so that my barns will be full.

I thank you Jesus for filling up my life. You make me complete and You fill every void! You are my heart and You are my worship. My life is not my own, but I belong to You. I am Yours and You are mine. I am Your bride. My body is Your temple. My soul longs for more of You.

Your word says when I cry out to You... You will answer me. Thank You for responding to me today Jesus. I praise You for I know You are at work behind the scenes and no devil in hell can stop YOU! There is a miracle in the making for me right now. I believe it and I receive it. In Jesus name I pray, AMEN!

PERSONAL THOUGHTS

Day 16

Jesus is My Focus

Matthew 14:29-30 (NLV)
Jesus said, "Come!" Peter got out of the boat and walked
on the water to Jesus. But when he saw the strong wind,
he was afraid. He began to go down in the water. He cried
out, "Lord, save me!"

I think it's amazing how Jesus is always asking us to "come" to where He is! So many times, we want Jesus to come to where we are. I am guilty too! I have prayed in times past for Jesus to come and help me, save me, and deliver me. But Jesus is asking us to come out to where He is. He will deliver you out of the storm if you would take the first step. If you take that first step out of the boat, you will get a different perspective. People in the boat only have the perspective from being in the boat. They cannot see what Jesus can see.

The first step is always hard, and It requires a lot of faith. Probably 1 out of 12 has enough faith to take such a step. But when that "one" finally decides to step out, he found out quickly it requires more faith to "STAY" than it did to step out.

In the boat Peter felt secure. In the boat Peter had friends with him. In the boat was the logical place to be.

Out of the boat, it was dark, lonely, and the waves seemed to have grown bigger. It was NOT the logical place to be. There was no security of a solid surface to walk on. Notice that none of his friends went with him, they were only spectators.

The pressure of stepping out was tough, but the faith to stay above water was even harder. He took a step and did good at first, because he was solely focused on Jesus in the middle of the storm. It took faith for him to step out, but look at this, the bible never said he was afraid to take the first step. It said he was afraid when he saw the strong wind. What!!! Didn't he know there was a strong wind before he stepped out? Of course, he did! The issue was not the strong wind, the issue was what he saw! When he stepped out, the bible says he saw Jesus and Jesus said to him, "come." It was when he lost his focus that he gave in to the pressure of the storm and he began to sink and cry for help.

Look at what Jesus said in verse 31:

> **At once Jesus put out His hand and took hold of him. Jesus said to Peter, "You have so little faith! Why did you doubt?"**

I think it's so amazing how Jesus saved him when he cried out. But I just wonder, what would have happened if Peter had not lost his focus? I mean, they were both walking on water at one point. I feel like Peter recognized as if Jesus was the power of sustaining him. The reason why Peter needed more faith to keep him is because the pressure was different outside the boat than it was inside the boat. When something is different, our human natures fights it. But when Jesus speaks to you "to come" He is speaking to your spirit, your heart, the very core of your being to follow Him, even if it requires walking through a strong storm, intense stress or pressure.

I feel like Jesus is saying in my heart right now to you, "I am calling you to come to the deep. I am calling you to do something you have never done before. The place I want to take you will require faith on a daily basis, each step of the way. You say to me, 'I can't, it's impossible!' But I am the God who performs miracles. Do you need a miracle? I can do it! Do you need provision? I can do it? Do you need a healing? I can do it? Whatever you need, I can do it. Don't be afraid to take the step and don't be afraid of the pressure and stress once you take it. Don't be afraid of the darkness. Don't be afraid of the solitude, it will not last forever. I will sustain you. I will keep you. Just keep your eyes on me and you will not fail, you will not falter, you will not sink, and you will not be destroyed. I will take you to places you've never been before. I will do more than you could ever imagine."

Can you imagine with me a minute? Let's imagine Peter as if he never took his eyes off Jesus. Where do you think they would've gone? What do you think would've happened next? When I imagine this, I see other disciples taking a step of faith (with my image maker), I see them forming a circle, connected to one another, watching as the strong wind subsides, rejoicing over the miracle that Jesus performed and worshipping Him. When your focus is on Jesus, the storm no longer has the power over you. Why is that? Because Jesus is your focus! Jesus has power over the storm!

We need to practice staying in peace!

From now on, Jesus is my FOCUS! In every situation, every circumstance, every heart break, every disappointment, every loss, every gain, every victory, every moment.

Jesus asked Peter to come out and walk on the water with HIM. The moment Peter lost his focus he began to drown. Do you feel like your drowning? If so, get your focus back. Set your eyes upon Jesus. In the storm, you will be able to walk on water. How about we start walking on water instead of drowning in fear and everything else!!!

Prayer:
Dear Jesus,
I love You, Lord with all my heart. You know my heart. You know when I doubt and when I am afraid. You know when I get just enough courage to take a step of faith, just to find myself crying out for You to save me. Lord, I want to go places with You that I have never gone before. I ask You to strengthen my heart and build my faith to believe You for miracles. Lord, You know right now that I need a miracle for You to do what You have put in my heart. I know that it will not be by might, nor my power, but by Your Spirit. It will be YOU. It has always been You pulling me through and bringing me out of a stinking, sinking mess. But today Lord, I pray for the faith to sustain me in the middle of stress, pressure, conflict, loneliness, and pain, not just to keep my head above water, but so that my feet will trod on the water. I believe it. I believe in miracles. I believe You are able to do anything. I will follow You. If you go to the deep, I will go to the deep. If You go to the left, I will go to the left. If you stay still, I will stay still. If You're walking on water, I will walk on water. I will only move when You

move. I will only speak when You speak. I declare with the images of my heart the possibilities of what this day can bring me when I believe You to perform it. My heart is steadfast upon You. I will lift my eyes to the hills where I know my HELP comes from. You are my Help. You are my everything. I will not lose my focus. Lord, help me not to lose my focus. In the name of Jesus Christ of Nazareth I pray, Amen!

PERSONAL THOUGHTS

_____

_____

_____

_____

_____

_____

_____

_____

_____

_____

_____

_____

_____

_____

_____

_____

_____

_____

_____

_____

_____

Day 17

Cast Away Comparison

Galatians 6:4
*Everyone should look at himself and see how he does his
own work. Then he can be happy in what he has done. He
should not compare himself with his neighbor.*

Comparison is deadly for the promises God has for you. It is deadly for
your destiny. It corrupts your soul.

When you compare yourself to another person or their possessions, you
are saying, "God, you did not do a good job writing my story, You did
better for my neighbor."

Then envy creeps in, like a LION, seeking an open door, to stir up conten-
tion, doubt, negativity, unbelief, and pain.

Envy says, "I want what I can't have!" it says, "I want my neighbors' job,
house, children, marriage, spouse!" It says, "I don't like my life and I want
my neighbor's life!"

Jeremiah 29:11 boldly says God has special plans, JUST FOR YOU! Designed for you! Especially for you! He says they are GOOD plans and for a
GOOD future and HE offers HOPE with it.

Psalm 139 says you are fearfully and wonderfully made. The prophetic
word was spoken by David declares God is writing your story. Satan does
not have permission to write your story. Your circumstances cannot write
your story. But your heavenly FATHER is writing your story. Your CRE-
ATOR! Trust HIM. He knows what is best for you!

James 3:14-16 *(ESV)*
*But if you have bitter jealousy and selfish ambition in
your hearts, do not boast and be false to the truth. This*

*is not the wisdom that comes down from above, but is
earthly, unspiritual, demonic. For where jealousy and
selfish ambition exist, there will be disorder and every vile
practice.*

In this passage you can see wisdom comes from ABOVE, in the Throne
Room of God, the Throne Room of Grace, and this is what you need to
conquer jealousy and envy. You need a Throne Room perspective of who
you are and of Whom you are!

It is only when you get rid of the root of "envy" and realize that comparison is a sin, then you will see the plans unfold for you.

Be at peace with WHO you are! Take a good look at your own life, your
own gifts, your own family, your own story, and you will find God in it. You
will find peace. Then do the work that Jesus is calling you to do. Nobody
else can do it like you!

Avoid "wishing" and "dreaming" of your neighbor's things! Create your
own!

Envy, jealousy and wishing for your neighbor's things only causes division
and grief and it will be the death of a relationship or dream.

> **1 Corinthians 3:1-4** *(ESV)*
> *But I, brothers, could not address you as spiritual people,
> but as people of the flesh, as infants in Christ. I fed you
> with milk, not solid food, for you were not ready for it.
> And even now you are not yet ready, for you are still of
> the flesh. For while there is **jealousy and strife among
> you**, are you not of the flesh and behaving only in a human
> way? For when one says, "I follow Paul," and another, "I
> follow Apollos," are you not being merely human?*

You may be asking yourself this, "Well, aren't I human?" Okay, yes, I get
it. You are human, but as a Christian, our behavior stems from our belief
system. What you truly believe about your God, yourself and others will
reflect somewhere in your relationships! Paul is emphasizing this: We

expect babies to act like babies, because that is what they are. But there comes a time as the baby grows, they will grow out of a certain pattern of behavior. It's the same way as Christians. When you first get saved, your behavior may still look like the World (a baby). But as you grow, your behavior changes because your perspective changes from a world view to a heavenly view!

Jealousy and envy will cause strife in a marriage, amongst siblings, with friendships, and in the work place.

Jealousy must be presented as a truth and a strong hold that is birthed from the pit of hell. Its purpose is to make you miserable, to hate yourself, to hate your life, and to hate others for what they have and for what you don't have!

The Word says in **Proverbs 16:3**

> *Commit to the Lord whatever **YOU** do, and **HE** will establish your plans.*

Notice HE didn't say, "commit to the Lord what your neighbor is doing... NO! He said Commit to **HIM** the work of your own hands, then and only then will **HE** establish your plans.

If you compare yourself with everyone else, or even with just one person, you are in danger of losing the promise that God has for you.

> "Comparison is the thief of joy."
> **- Theodore Roosevelt**

Think on this:

> **1 Thessalonians 4:11-12**
> *... that you also aspire to lead a quiet life, to mind your own business, and to work with your own hands, as we commanded you, that you may walk properly toward those who are outside, and that you may **lack nothing**.*

In other words:

- Take a good look at your own life
- Mind your own business
- Do your own work to the fullness
- Walk properly among non-believers (Non-Christians)

Then you WILL LACK NOTHING!

There is nothing more satisfying than saying at the end of the day, "I have worked hard, I am working towards my dreams, I am giving all my work to the Lord Jesus, I am committing my family to Jesus, I am at peace with the results of my work today!"

Try it!! It feels much better than comparing yourself, and your dreams with your neighbor's.

Here is what you must do to get rid of it:

- Realize you struggle with it and be honest with yourself
- Realize where it comes from
- Repent and turn from this behavior
- Ask God to give you a brand-new perspective of your own life
- Stay focused on Jesus and keep your eyes off other people and what they have
- Do not compare, this is very dangerous
- Realize comparison is rooted in envy
- Be at peace with who you are, and the WAY God is writing your story
- Love yourself, love your life, love your God, and love your neighbor
- Live each day as a new day, with new possibilities and new revelations from God.

> ### 2 Corinthians 10:12 (ESV)
> *Not that we dare to classify or compare ourselves with some of those who are commending themselves. But when they measure themselves by one another and compare themselves with one another, they are without understanding.*

Prayer:

Dear Father,

I thank you for Your Word! It is mighty and powerful for the pulling down of strongholds! I pray in the name of Jesus, every stronghold of envy and comparison is BROKEN, right now, in my life! In the name of Jesus, I release in the atmosphere the spirit of peace, joy and contentment in my home, in my work place, in my family, in my church and in my soul. I expose the lies of the enemy that says, "We lack resources, or we lack talent, or we lack anything that will cause me to envy and compare!" I repent for not being content with my life and the things You have put in my life. You made no mistakes when You created me. You have equipped me, and I am well able to do what You have put in me. Help me find my lane and stay in my lane and not to desire to be in someone else's lane. Your Word says You will finish the perfect work you have started in me for all the days of my life. I will now rest in the fact that You made no mistakes and I am fearfully and wonderfully made, and I declare with a loud voice I am free from all envy and jealousy!

Now, I ask you Jesus, to FILL UP MY LIFE with your powerful LOVE! I know and understand Your powerful, unfailing, unswerving love will cast off every symptom of comparison! Wrap Your loving arms around me oh Lord! Reveal Your PERFECT PLANS for me that can only be done by You… for such a time as this… I speak and declare the plans of the Lord will be established here on earth as it is in HEAVEN! IN JESUS NAME! AMEN!

PERSONAL THOUGHTS

_____

_____

_____

_____

_____

_____

_____

_____

_____

Day 18

Don't Die With Your Treasure

James 1:17 (NKJV)
*Every good gift and every perfect gift is from **above**, and comes **down** from the Father of lights, with whom there is no variation or shadow of turning.*

The Word of God declares that every good gift comes from above, the Throne Room of God! He deposits in you as it is coming down, from the Father, who is the Author of your life. Every person has been handed a gift.

Jesus explained it in a parable of the talents like this:

Matthew 25:14-30 (NKJV)
The Parable of the Talents
"For the kingdom of heaven is like a man traveling to a far country, who called his own servants and delivered his goods to them. And to one he gave five talents, to another two, and to another one, to each according to his own ability; and immediately he went on a journey. Then he who had received the five talents went and traded with them and made another five talents. And likewise, he who had received two gained two more also. But he who had received one went and dug in the ground and hid his lord's money. After a long time the lord of those servants came and settled accounts with them. "So, he who had received five talents came and brought five other talents, saying, 'Lord, you delivered to me five talents; look, I have gained five more talents besides them.' His lord said to him, 'Well done, good and faithful servant; you were faithful over a few things, I will make you ruler over many things. Enter into the joy of your lord.' He also who had received

two talents came and said, 'Lord, you delivered to me
two talents; look, I have gained two more talents besides
them.' His lord said to him, 'Well done, good and faithful
servant; you have been faithful over a few things, I will
make you ruler over many things. Enter into the joy of your
lord.'

"Then he who had received the one talent came and
said, 'Lord, I knew you to be a hard man, reaping where
you have not sown, and gathering where you have not
scattered seed. And I was afraid and went and hid your
talent in the ground. Look, there you have what is yours.'
"But his lord answered and said to him, 'You wicked and
lazy servant, you knew that I reap where I have not sown
and gather where I have not scattered seed. So you ought
to have deposited my money with the bankers, and at my
coming I would have received back my own with interest.
So, take the talent from him and give it to him who has ten
talents.

'For to everyone who has, more will be given, and he will
have abundance; but from him who does not have, even
what he has will be taken away. And cast the unprofitable
servant into the outer darkness. There will be weeping and
gnashing of teeth.'

It is a sad thing when you bury your gift because of fear and comparison.
It is even worse when you die with your gift and never did anything with it.

We all have driven past cemeteries. You will see beautiful carved tomb-
stones. You will see beautiful flowers loved ones have put on the grave. I
have been to cemeteries with thousands of graves. I believe the wealthiest
place on earth is the graveyard. It's not the oil fields of Iraq or the diamond
mines of Africa. You may be asking, "Why is the graveyard the wealthiest
place on earth?" Because buried in the cemetery are dreams that were
never fulfilled, gifts that were never used, and talents that were buried in
the grave of the heart.

There are ideas in the cemetery that never came to pass. There are visions that never came to pass. There are books never written. There are songs never sung. There are inventions never designed. There are sermons never preached. There are architects never built. The cemetery is FULL of unused treasure!

Is it possible that you could add to the treasure of the grave?

Buried in the cemetery is treasure that makes God weep! Buried inside of you are God-given dreams and you are supposed to accomplish them while you are here on earth.

There are things God has planted in your heart that you have not even done yet. This is my prayer for you! Don't die with your treasure. Don't die without trying! Go back and rob the grave of what belongs to you. It was given by God. It was written in heaven. The Throne Room of God has the resources you need to make it come to pass. You need to die empty, not full of treasure! You need to accomplish all that God has put in YOU!

You have God-given potential. Potential is: untapped power, unused ability, dormant strength, hidden power, all you could be, but you haven't become it yet, all you can do, but you haven't done it yet.

Potential is never what you have done, it is always what you could do, but you haven't done it yet.

Whenever you've done something it is no longer your potential. Potential is everything yet unused, but yet still within you!

Never allow what you have done to keep you from what you could do.

> **Ephesians 1:3** *(AMPC)*
> *May blessing (praise, laudation, and eulogy) be to the God and Father of our Lord Jesus Christ (the Messiah) Who has blessed us in Christ with every spiritual (given by the Holy Spirit) blessing in the heavenly realm!*

Remember: *Every good gift and every perfect gift is from* **above**, *and comes* **down** *from the Father.*

The gifts you have comes from ABOVE and it came down to you by the

Father and your gift has so much potential to multiply if you don't bury it. We can avoid burying it if you stop comparing your gifts to other people. When you compare, it kills, and when something is dead, you bury it. This is very hurtful to God. You have to understand the devil hates you and he wants to rob you of all the potential you have and discourage you from tapping into your God-given potential, so you will die full of treasure and not empty.

How can you discover your treasure? You must know and understand there is freedom in knowledge and truth. The key to truth is Jesus and your focus on Him and not on judging and comparing man.

The greatest enemy to man is not sin, or Satan, but it is ignorance!

> **Hosea 4:6** *(AMPC)*
> *My people are destroyed for lack of knowledge; because you [the priestly nation] have rejected knowledge, I will also reject you that you shall be no priest to Me; seeing you have forgotten the law of your God, I will also forget your children.*

Why reject the children? Because you can only teach them what you know. To stay ignorant is a decision! Knowledge is the key to freedom. But the key *to knowledge is* TRUTH!

We think knowledge is POWER! That is not necessarily true! Because you can learn the wrong thing.

Jesus said the only thing that can set you free is TRUTH.

> **John 8:32**
> *And you will know the Truth,*
> *and the Truth will set you free.*

IT IS DANGEROUS TO LEARN THE WRONG THING! Some people are experts in error! Knowledge doesn't' mean you are smart, because what you have learned may not be true.

IT IS DANGEROUS TO BELIEVE SOMETHING TO BE TRUE, WHEN IT IS NOT!

I ask myself this question every day, "Lord, show me truth, and help me to change what I believe to be true to what is actually true!"

It is a mess to have great zeal and to speak and believe in error. Look at this and think about it a minute. Probably many of your wounds from the past is from believing something in error. God is not so much concerned with our behavior as He is with what we BELIEVE. Your life will follow what you believe! If you believe a lie, then your journey here on earth will be a lie.

Hitler, believed that everybody else was subhuman, and his race was superior. This FALSE BELIEF made him massacre millions of people. It is dangerous to believe the wrong thing!!!!

The key to truth is Jesus. He is your creator. He is your manufacturer. The manufacturer is the only one who knows the truth about his product. Everybody else is just experimenting it and guessing it and having a strong opinion about it. That is why you need to get your information from the manufacturer, your creator, JESUS! Don't even believe the retailor, because he is in it for the sales. This is why you can't trust people to tell you who you are! You have to find out who you are in Christ Jesus. Don't depend other's opinion of you and their one-on one experience with you to determine your value.

The manufacturer knows, if you don't read the manual careful, you can do more harm than good. You get your instructions from the Word of God. The Bible is your manual.

Have you ever tried to put something together without reading the instructions first? Of course not, only your spouse does that!

I have a "Smart TV" and it can perform numerous things, but you know what? I have no clue how to do it! Does that mean it's a bad product? No! It means I need to take some time to sit down and read how wonderful this product can be if I knew how to operate it. I am limiting myself by trying to figure it out and learn two or three functions it has without tapping in to all that it was created to do. You know exactly where I am going with this, don't you?

Open the Bible and read it for yourself! Find out what God says about you, then believe Him when He says it. Your life will follow what you believe to be true!

The manual is the Word of God! It gives you instructions and truth about the Maker and His product!

MANU is a Latin word, "to make" or "maker." Manufacturer means the "Maker's Mind."

What the Maker did was take His mind and put it on paper and sent it with the product so when you read it, you are reading His mind about the product. He is saying, "Hey you! Don't attempt to operate this product until you read My mind completely!"

Why? Because, He designed you, He put you together and He knows how you operate and function! He knows all the potential that is inside you.

When God made you, He made no mistakes about you. He deposited in you certain gifts and talents. He knows what you are capable of. He has a magnificent plan! When He created you, He had a purpose in mind.

A few years ago, we used to have a Motif Electric Piano. Back then, it was the latest thing out and it could do so many cool things. But in order to know how to use it, we had to read the mind of the manufacturer. It's called the Instruction Manuel. But then came along a newer, better piano called the Nord 2. It is so complicated! I could barely turn it on and off! But the potential this piano has exceeds all the rest! The instructions start off like this: Let's take a few minutes to get acquainted with your new Nord 2! Then two hours later… it was more than a few minutes. Honestly, I am still learning this piano. But the more time I spend with it and reading the directions, eventually I will master it.

It is the same way with God. The more time we spend with Him and reading His Mind, (the Word) eventually, we will get it! When we get it is when we start multiplying! In **Psalm 139** David knew His Maker! He said, "Lord I praise You, for I am fearfully and wonderfully made. You knitted me together in my mother's womb, You know me! And I know full well that your works are wonderful!" Paraphrased by me!

If you are white, he wanted you white. If you are black, He wanted you black. If you are mixed, He wanted you mixed. Whoever you are and where ever you came from, God did it, He is your Maker, He is your Builder, He is your manufacturer.

YOU ARE PERFECT FOR WHAT YOU WERE BORN TO DO!

Remember, with the Lord, ALL THINGS ARE POSSIBLE. You are chosen to do great things and BECOME great! Make no mistake about it!

> **Ephesians 1:4** *(AMPC)*
> *Even as [in His love] He chose us [actually picked us out for Himself as His own] in Christ before the foundation of the world, that we should be holy (consecrated and set apart for Him) and blameless in His sight, even above reproach, before Him in love.*

You have work to do on the earth! You have treasure in You. Don't die buried with your treasure. Stop regretting your past and start working on your future. He chose you! He loves you! He has GREAT PLANS FOR YOU! Just because you see a sign that says "DETOUR," don't get mad and go back to the old way and end the journey. Keep moving forward! You may get re-routed, it may take a little longer, but you will arrive at the destination if you keep moving forward! Let's get busy living instead of dying.

Prayer:

Dear Lord,

I know You are not playing games with my life. I know You have already determined the end from the beginning. You have brought me here because there is an assignment from You for me to do! You have already seen the end of it. I know You are working out all the bad stuff, the mistakes, failures, lies, heart-aches and frustrations. You see my complications and You have resources for my walk here on earth. You know the direction You want to take with my purpose and You are making every crooked road straight! I declare in the name of Jesus, I am strong when I am weak, and I will finish my race using every gift You have given me! I will not die full of gifts never used. But as I live, I will tap in to my God-given potential and do everything You have planned for me. I will not complain!

I will not doubt! I will not beat myself up when I feel like I make mistakes. But I will daily come to Your Throne Room to receive grace, to receive forgiveness, to receive strength, to receive power, to receive revelation, to receive ideas, to receive love and knowledge that comes from above. I know the enemy comes to kill, still and destroy, but You are more powerful than the enemy. You are my God and You are my life. Your Manuel tells me I can do ALL things through Jesus who gives me strength. I will not quit. I will not turn back. But I will finish strong. I will not wait for the enemy to stop attacking me, because I realize Satan will never let up! But I am confident You will take what the enemy means for harm to sling me into my destiny! Just like the stone in the hands of David had the potential to kill Goliath, I am in the same way, in your hands with much potential to conquer everything that gets in my way and to do great things. Lord, forgive me for comparing myself to others and making the focus about me, and what I have or don't have. But now, I set my focus on You in the Throne Room and I am content and completely satisfied with the gifts and talents You have given me. You and I together will conquer every foe! And I declare I will finish strong, In Jesus Name!

PERSONAL THOUGHTS

Day 19

When God Writes Upon My Heart

Psalm 139:16
Your eyes saw my unformed body; all the days ordained
for me were written in your book before one of them came
to be.

God is writing the story of our life.
He writes the plans He has for us: *Jeremiah 29:11*
He writes our names in the lamb's book of life: *Revelation 13:8*
Our name is written on the palm of His hand: *Isaiah 49:1*

The question is: What is He writing? What is He planning? What is God up to? Why did He say he was writing our days out?

God is organized, and He has a great plan and He wants you and me to be able to know what His plan is. When we live from "heaven to earth" we can find out what His perfect plan is for our life. We find it by reading the Bible, abiding in His presence and feeling His desires He has put in our heart.

Listen to what David said in *Psalm 139* and he writes in detail about the thoughts God has towards us and His loving-kindness.

Psalm 139 (NIV)
You have searched me, Lord, and you know me.
You know when I sit and when I rise; you perceive my
thoughts from afar.
You discern my going out and my lying down; you are
familiar with all my ways.
Before a word is on my tongue you, Lord, know it
completely.

You hem me in behind and before, and you lay your hand upon me.

Such knowledge is too wonderful for me, too lofty for me to attain.

Where can I go from your Spirit? Where can I flee from your presence?

If I go up to the heavens, you are there; if I make my bed in the depths, you are there.

If I rise on the wings of the dawn, if I settle on the far side of the sea,

even there your hand will guide me, your right hand will hold me fast.

If I say, "Surely the darkness will hide me, and the light become night around me,"

even the darkness will not be dark to you; the night will shine like the day,

for darkness is as light to you.

For you created my inmost being; you knit me together in my mother's womb.

I praise you because I am fearfully and wonderfully made; your works are wonderful,

I know that full well.

My frame was not hidden from you when I was made in the secret place,

when I was woven together in the depths of the earth.

*Your eyes saw my unformed body; **all the days ordained for me were written in your book** before one of them came to be.*

How precious to me are your thoughts, God! How vast is the sum of them!

WHEN GOD WRITES UPON MY HEART

From the beginning of your life, according to verse 16, your days were written out. Here we can see that God is the Author of your life. In *Hebrews 12:2* it says we ought to LOOK to JESUS who is the **Author** and **Finisher** of our faith. We should not look to physics, horoscopes, or the stars for advice about the story line of our life. But we should look solely to JESUS. He is writing our story. We have to be okay with the story line HE is writing. All the good, bad and the ugly have a divine purpose. Just to make one thing clear. God doesn't design tragedy in your life. All things that pertain to killing, stealing and destroying is all by Satan himself. This is his main purpose. However, God saw it first, then He wrote it, then He responded to it as HE became your HELP. I have seen God use the dark places of my life to push me into my destiny and make me the person I am today.

So, now let's take a look at the script of your life to see what God is writing upon your heart.

First, God will put a dream in your heart. Let's take a look.

1. Dreams

What are your dreams? What are your desires? What is God speaking to you about? Is God speaking to you, or should I say, Can you hear Him speaking to you?

Look at the story line of these people!

Joseph had a dream… his dream went from vision to pit, from pit to slavery, from slavery to prison, from prison to palace, then in the palace he saw his dream come to pass…

David felt God writing upon his heart… he was on the back side of the desert, abandoned, forgotten, lonely, but yet in preparation… he was writing songs, hymns, fighting lions and bears just to find himself faced with a prophet one day who said he would be king… then he faced a giant and killed it, he was promoted from desert to war, from war to worship leading and casting out evil spirits, he went from leading worship to leading war, then he found himself in the position of a King and the prophecy, the dream, came to pass…

Daniel dreamed, and as he dreamed , he wrote... God showed him end times and all the things that were to come... just to find himself in a lion's den, yet God was not finished with his story, he sent an angel to save him, and the result was that Daniel made God's name famous all over the land...

Esther had a purpose, as God was writing her story, she found herself an orphan, whether she was abandoned or parents killed, she was being raised by her Uncle... her inward beauty radiated from the out-side and caused her to be chosen for Queen... meanwhile, it was her Uncle who pushed her to greatness, he was ordained and anointed by God to pour into her life. All the dark places of her life led her to a place and a time designated and written by God to save her and her people.... God all the while was WRITING UPON HER HEART... and HER UNCLE!

Just in the same way that Joseph and Daniel dreamed, you too, have dreams... and in the same way that David and Esther had impressions upon their heart, God is writing a dream upon your heart even as you read this passage.

When you have a dream and you know your purpose, you should write it down! Let's take a look at Habakkuk's dream, complaint and resolution.

2. Write the Vision Down

Habakkuk's Complaint

Habakkuk 1 *(NIV)*

The prophecy that Habakkuk the prophet received. How long, Lord, must I call for help, but you do not listen? Or cry out to you, "Violence!" but you do not save? Why do you make me look at injustice? Why do you tolerate wrongdoing...

The Lord's Answer

"Look at the nations and watch–and be utterly amazed. For I am going to do something in your days that you would not believe, even if you were told... "

Habakkuk's Second Complaint

Lord, are you not from everlasting? My God, my Holy One,
you will never die.
You, Lord, have appointed them to execute judgment... Is
he to keep on emptying his net, destroying nations without
mercy?

He ends his complaint with a question... then... there is no answer,
but silence...

Then Habakkuk writes this in Chapter 2

Habakkuk 2 *(NIV)*
I will stand at my watch and station myself on the
ramparts;
I will look to see what HE will say to me, and what answer I
am to give to this complaint

The Lord's Answer, His Resolution

*Then the Lord replied: "**Write down the revelation** and*
***make it plain** on tablets so that a herald may **run with it**.*
*For the revelation awaits **an appointed time**; it speaks of*
*the end and will not prove false. **Though it linger, wait for**
***it; it will certainly come** and will not delay.*

So, God spoke to him and said, "Hey Habakkuk, I know the plans I
have for you. And I have a perfect timing for it. But there is something
I need for YOU TO DO! **WRITE YOUR DREAM DOWN**! Keep it before
YOU because I have a perfect time to cause it to come to pass!"

God ordained for him to write, wait & worship!

Look how God spoke to others to WRITE!

Jeremiah 30:2 *(NIV)*
*"This is what the Lord, the God of Israel, says: '**Write in a**
***book** all the words I have spoken to you.*

Proverbs 3:3 *(NIV)*
*Let love and faithfulness never leave you; bind them around your neck, **write them on the tablet of your heart**.*

Luke 1:3 *(NIV)*
*With this in mind, since I myself have carefully investigated everything from the beginning, I too decided **to write** an orderly account for you,*

Joshua 24:26 *(NKJV)*
*Then Joshua **wrote these words** in the Book of the Law of God*

Deuteronomy 6:9 *(NKJV)*
*You shall **write them** on the doorposts of your house and on your gates.*

Revelation 1:11 *(NKJV)*
*saying, "I am the Alpha and the Omega, the First and the Last," and, "What you see, **write in a book** and send it to the seven churches*

Hebrews 8:10 *(NKJV)*
*For this is the covenant that I will make with the house of Israel after those days, says the Lord: I will put My laws in their mind and **write them on their hearts**; and I will be their God, and they shall be My people.*

This is what Psychologists say about writing things down:

- Writing things down is a key to effectiveness.

  It helps you free up your mind, think on paper, and better organize your thoughts.

- If you don't write things down, your mind spends more time "paper shuffling" and creates its own anxiety.

10 Reasons to Write Things Down

Why write things down? Here are some key insights and reminders:

- **Your mind lies.** Your mind easily distorts things. That's a blessing and a curse. If you write things down, you change perspective. Now you are looking at it on paper. Does it still make the same sense as it did in your head?

- **Think on paper.** When it's on paper, you can look your challenges in the eyes, and slice them down to size. Your mind is a powerful thing when it can more objectively look at things instead of swirling them around in your head.

- **Organize your thoughts.** To write things down, you have to think a little bit to find the words or to figure out what it means. Right off the bat, the act of trying to write something down shapes your thoughts. Once it's down on paper, you can now list things in a way that helps you think.

- **It sinks in better.** Writing it down creates a little more of an experience, and that helps it stick.

- **Free up your mind.** When you write something down, you free up the task of having to remember it. That might not sound like a big deal when it's just a few things, but you might spend your mind on better things. And, just imagine when it's more than a few things, and it's lots of things on your mind.

- **Calm your mind.** The Zeigarnik Effect says we tend to hang on to things in our mind, if we don't finish what we start. If you write things down, you free up your mind from worrying about what you forgot or what you need to remember.

- **Let things go.** You can let things naturally slough off by squeezing them out with better things to focus on. You can also more deliberately let things go, or simply cut them, because now you have a bird's-eye view. Decide what matters and what doesn't. Let things go that don't matter

- **Avoid task saturation.** Write things down to avoid task saturation. Three signs of task saturation are shutting down, compartmentalizing, and channelizing. Shutting down is when you simply stop performing. Compartmentalizing and channelizing is when you act busy, but all your doing is organizing and reorganizing lists and doing things sequentially, but not actually producing effective results.

- **Rehydrate ideas.** You can rehydrate your ideas later on as you need them.

- **Shelve things.** You can put things on the shelf to worry about at a later time.

When You have a dream and you know your purpose, you should write it down. When you start writing it down, it says, "I believe this is going to happen!" Then you need to get ready for a change, a shift!

3. **Get Ready For Change**
   (I will be quoting from Day 3 and Day 5 of "The Book of Mysteries" & Day 5 by Jonathan Cahn)

   The Shannah & Manah

Day 3 Quote [a]

"What is a year… 365 days? It is more than just 365. It's called **shannah** and it contains a secret. It is linked to the number two. **Shannah** can mean the second, the duplicate or the repeat. In the course of nature the year is the repeating of what has already been. The winter, the spring, the summer and the fall, the blossoming of flowers and their withering away, the rebirth of nature and it's dying, the same progression, the same replaying of what already was. So a year is a **shannah**, a repetition. And now you have a new year before you, so what kind of year will it be? The nature of nature is to repeat, just as we live, by nature, as creatures of habit. We gravitate toward doing that which we've done before, the same routines and courses, even when those routines are harmful to us.

But you have a choice! You see, **shannah** has a double meaning. It not only means the repeat… it also means the change. The way of the world is to repeat, but the way of God is the way of newness and

[a] "Day 3." The Book of Mysteries, by Jonathan Cahn, FrontLine, 2016.

change. You can't know God and not be changed by knowing Him."

Day 5 Quote [b]

"Today we will speak of the days before you. What will the days yet to come bring to your life! It is written to number your days. It means our days are limited, and so it's wise to number them. But in the original language is a secret. And this secret can change your life, the days of your life. In the Hebrew it says, teach us to *manah* our days. *Manah* means more than just number. It means to prepare and to appoint. So you must not only number your days, you must learn to prepare your days, to appoint your days. You don't just watch passively and wait to see what your days will bring. You are to prepare them!"

These two passages changed my life!

You must make changes throughout the year and be careful not to repeat the same ole thing. If you keep doing the same ole thing, you will keep getting the same ole results.

- You must think about each day and play, prepare and appoint! Make an appointment with your destiny, and keep it by showing up!!

  Psalm 90:12 (NKJV)
  So teach us to number our days, that we may gain a heart of wisdom.

  Acts 19:21 (NKJV)
  *When these things were accomplished, Paul **purposed in the Spirit**, when he had passed through Macedonia and Achaia, to go to Jerusalem, saying, "After I have been there, I must also see Rome."*
  I want to share a scripture with you I have read for years, but just recently had a sweet revelation from...

  Ephesians 3:20 (NIV)
  *Now to him who is able to do immeasurably more than all we ask or **imagine**, according to his power that **is at work within us**...*

[b] "Day 5." The Book of Mysteries, by Jonathan Cahn, FrontLine, 2016.

The Power that is in work in you is the same Power that raised Jesus Christ from the dead. You have resurrection Power that lives in you and works in you. If you can imagine it, He can do it. To imagine is to have an image in your heart of what you are asking for.

If you are asking for God to heal your marriage, then begin to imagine what a healthy marriage looks like. If you are asking God to heal your body, then begin to imagine what a healthy body looks like. If you are asking God to help you lose weight, then begin to imagine what a skinny body looks like! If you are asking God to touch your finances and to increase them, then begin to draw the images on your heart of what it looks like. If you have a dream, ask God to give you the desires of your heart. Not evil desires, but HIS desires and you will see God write HIS dreams upon your heart, so you will carry out His plan for your life, here on earth as it is in heaven.

Not only do you imagine it and see it, but you put it before you on a daily basis, and you write it down on daily basis. When you write it down, God said to Habakkuk, that it may tarry, but run with the vision anyway, and wait for it because it will come to pass when the timing has been set and then it will not delay.

When God writes upon your heart, there is no devil in hell that can stop you and God's dream for you (together as a team).

Remember this: when you face storms, and trials and persecution, and you feel like "all of hell" is coming against you, understand and acknowledge Jesus and ask Him to open the eyes of your heart to see what you can see in the storm. You will see indeed that it is not "all of hell" coming against you, but when God writes upon your heart, and you begin to walk out your dreams, it is YOU and Jesus coming against all of hell!

You will feel the heat from hell, you will feel the pain from it, but it will not harm you. Now, in my heart, when I experience a trial, I never say that hell is coming against me, I just say that I am coming against all of hell. I must be doing something amazing and God must be at work IN ME! The devil is scared of the resurrection power that lives in you and me.

Prayer:

Dear Abba Father,

Today my Lord, I open my heart to You. I ask You to put Your dreams in my heart You have for me. Create in me a clean heart and a heart that is after You. Lord, my soul longs for You and more of You in my life. I can feel You writing upon my heart today. I ask You to erase all the pain from my past that I've been holding in my soul. All the disappointment, all the hurt and betrayal from friends and family. I know I am not alone, but You are with me. Help me to see the plans you have for me, so I can walk them out according to your perfect will. Not my will, but let Your will be done in my life and for my family, here on earth as it is in heaven. As You have written for me, on the day I was born, so be it, all the days of my life, just as you have said. Help me Lord not to repeat the same mistakes of last year but help me to change and to do something different. Help me to prepare my days. Help me to appoint my days. Help me to make an appointment with my destiny! Help me to write things down! Help me to remember each day is a blessing and not take my days here on earth for granted. I declare that my best years are ahead of me and not behind me. I will reach towards Your Throne Room and find my help and strength for every day.

Lord, I trust You with the story line of my life. When things do not make sense, I trust You, when it looks like a tornado has torn through my life, and I feel alone, I trust You and the story You are writing.

Thank You for the resurrection Power that lives in me and helps me along life's way. Today my Lord, I make a strong declaration of love towards You and trust. I love You and trust You. I acknowledge You at work in me, therefore, no harm will come to me. You are my guide, You are my shield, You are my Shepherd, You are my everything Lord. Thank You for loving me and taking good care of me. Thank You for writing upon my heart. In Jesus Name, Amen.

PERSONAL THOUGHTS

Day 20

When Faith Is Connected To My Dream

> *Ephesians 3:20 (NIV)*
> *Now to him who is able to do immeasurably more than all*
> *we ask or **imagine**, according to his power that **is at work***
> ***within us**...*

To imagine: means to form a mental image. God said He made us in HIS image. That word image, when traced back to the Hebrew, actually means heart. When He made you, not only had He formed a mental image but He saw you with His heart.

> *Genesis 1:27 (NKJV)*
> *So, God created man in His own image; in the image of*
> *God He created him; male and female He created them.*

Look at it like this: God created man with His own imagination: in the HEART of God, He created male and female.

Our imagination is powerful! God is the ONE who made our imagination. But the devil loves to use our imagination to show us what his will is. He loves to give you dreams that are filled with fear and torture. He loves making horror movies that starts first in the imagination of producer. He loves creating arguments first that come through presumptions created by our imagination.

Look at what God says about this!

> *2 Corinthians 10:4-7 (NKJV)*
> *For the weapons of our warfare are not carnal but mighty*
> *in God for pulling down strongholds, casting down*
> *arguments and every high thing that exalts itself against*
> *the knowledge of God, bringing every thought into*
> *captivity to the obedience of Christ, and being ready to*
> *punish all disobedience when your obedience is fulfilled.*

When we don't cast them down, we let strongholds build in our mind, in our heart and in our imagination. Then we begin to respond to them. But the Word says we should bring EVERY thought into captivity. We should build a wall around every thought and analyze where the thought came from. You will know when it comes from hell. It feels heavy, depressing, painful, dreadful, and dirty. The Word says to cast them down, resist the devil and he will flee.

But what can happen to YOU if you use your imagination when connected to the will of God in heaven?

> ### Ephesians 3:20 (NIV)
> *Now to him who is able to do immeasurably more than all we ask or **imagine**, according to his power that **is at work within us**...*
>
> ### Acts 19:21 (NKJV)
> *When these things were accomplished, Paul **purposed in the Spirit**, when he had passed through Macedonia and Achaia, to go to Jerusalem, saying, "After I have been there, I must also see Rome."*

God made you on purpose. You are not a mistake. God has a dream for your life. God has a plan for your life. God's dreams are big for you. He wants you to partner with HIM and come into agreement of all that He wants for you.

Paul's dream was to deliver the gospel of Jesus Christ to the World. He knew if he could reach Rome he would be able to accomplish his dream. So, the Word says **He purposed in his spirit** to go to Jerusalem, then to Rome.

When you start to dream, you will write like Habakkuk. Then you will worship as you wait. Waiting is always the hard part and that's where faith steps in. Let's see what happens now when faith is connected to your dream.

Faith is the substance of things HOPED for (seen in the heart) and the evidence not seen (in the natural circumstance).

It takes Faith to see a dream fulfilled

Three things you must do while you wait! or hope for your dream.

1. **Have Faith:** take responsibility for your part! Stay in agreement with God's promise with your words, your walk, your talk, your actions, and with your belief.

    > *James 2:14-26 (NKJV)*
    > *What does it profit, my brethren, if someone says he has faith but does not have works? Can faith save him? If a brother or sister is naked and destitute of daily food, and one of you says to them, "Depart in peace, be warmed and filled," but you do not give them the things which are needed for the body, what does it profit? Thus also faith by itself, if it does not have works, is dead.*
    > *But someone will say, "You have faith, and I have works." Show me your faith without your works, and I will show you my faith by my works. You believe that there is one God. You do well.* **Even the demons believe**—*and tremble! But do you want to know, O foolish man, that faith without works is dead? ... [And the Scripture was fulfilled which says,* **"Abraham believed God... For as the body without the spirit is dead, so faith without works is dead also.***]*

I want to introduce to you a word in Hebrew

The word Emun speaks of that which is sure, solid, and true. If you add "ah" to it, it becomes Emunah. This is where we get our word "amen" from. "Emun" actually sounds like "amen."

Emunah is the Hebrew word for FAITH. Therefore, faith is linked to truth.

Faith is linked to that which is rock solid, the truth! Faith is that which you join yourself, root yourself, and ground yourself to the truth.

And the word **_Emunah_** also means steadfast, established, stable, and steady. The truer faith you have, the more steadfast you become, the more stable, the steadier, and the more established.

Colossians 2:6-7 (NKJV)
*As you therefore have received Christ Jesus the Lord, so walk in Him, **rooted** and built up in Him and **established** in the **faith**, as you have been taught, abounding in it with thanksgiving.*

1 Peter 5:8-10
*Be sober and vigilant. Your opponent the devil is prowling around like a roaring lion looking for [someone] to devour. Resist him, **steadfast** in **faith**, knowing that your fellow believers throughout the world undergo the same sufferings. The God of all grace who called you to his eternal glory through Christ [Jesus] will himself **restore**, **confirm**, **strengthen**, and **establish** you after you have suffered a little.*

Ephesians 3:17 (NKJV)
*that Christ may dwell in your hearts through **faith**; that you, being **rooted** and **grounded** in love...*

1 Corinthians 16:13 (NIVUK)
*Be on your guard; **stand firm** in the **faith**; be **courageous**; be **strong**.*

Faith causes you to become strong.

The word **AMEN** also comes from the word **Emun**. So to say AMEN is to say, "it's true, I agree, yes!"

So, what is faith?

Faith is to give your amen to God's Emun! His truth![a]
(Quoted from "The Book of Mysteries" by Jonathan Cahn)

Faith is to say amen, yes to God, amen to His reality, amen to His love, and amen to His salvation... not just with your mouth, but with your heart, your mind, your emotions, your strength, your words, your actions, your imagination and your life.

[a] *"Day 26." The Book of Mysteries, by Jonathan Cahn, FrontLine, 2016.*

Having real faith says, "I am anchored to my promise.

It cannot be separated from me!

I am anchored to my destiny, I am anchored to every promise in the Word of God.

It is a part of who I am! I am anchored to love.

I am anchored to strength! I am anchored to Jesus!"

2.   **Begin your dream with the end in mind:**

> *Isaiah 46:10 (NKJV)*
> *Remember the former things of old, For I am God, and there is no other;*
> *I am God, and there is none like Me, **Declaring the end from the beginning**...*

While you wait, you declare & define your purpose and mission in life, in your marriage, in your children, in your business, in your finances, in your health. Have you ever just took a few minutes to IMAGINE what the END of your dream/vision looks like?

Set your goals. See the big picture then see the details later. Details come week by week and month by month.

> *Philippians 3:13-15*
> *Brothers and sisters, I do not consider myself yet to have taken hold of it. But one thing I do: forgetting what is behind and straining toward what is ahead. I **press** on **toward the goal** to win the prize for which God has called me heavenward in Christ Jesus. All of us, then, who are mature **should take such a view of things**...*

Be careful to not speak death, but to speak life.

Be Responsible for your life, your behavior, and your language.

Instead of getting angry and saying things you regret and your language turns dark... take a moment to breath, stop, look, and listen.

Then remain calm and think like the little choo choo who could.

Avoid whining and complaining and turn your language from fault finding and fault blaming to, "I am sorry, or I was wrong" and instead of focusing on the problem, **focus on the solution**.

First seek to understand then be understood! Take responsibility for your attitude, your language, and your actions.

In the middle of conflict, discouragement, or arguments, learn to respond from your Spirit (where the truth is) and not from your soul (where the hurt is).

The soul will remind you of all the negatives and the past

The Spirit will remind you of your future and your goals and He will help bring you back into focus and give you strength to keep pressing

Take a moment to look inward and ask yourself: Am I living in the past by my words and actions?

I want to take a moment to remind you: you are not a victim, but you are victorious, you are head and not the tail, you are blessed and highly favored, you are humble, you are kind and courteous, you are a child of the King, you are capable of overcoming. You have what it takes to do this.

If you do not stop and take a moment to evaluate, write things down, you will find yourself looking at the past, by default, then repeating the past in your future.

- What do I need to accomplish today?
- What do I need to accomplish for this week?
- What do I need to accomplish for the month?
- What do I need to accomplish for the year?
- What do I need to accomplish in my life?

Go Backwards, then work your way up by this list:

We need to live each day with a goal (end results) in mind by faith, being rooted, immoveable, unshakeable, saying:

- God knows my end from the beginning

- He is working all things together for my good

- Thou I walk through the valley of Shadow of death, I will fear no evil.

- When I am weak He is strong

- His right hand upholds me

- His Holy Spirit lives in me and is leading me and directing me

- I am not alone, God is with me

- If God is for me, who can be against me

- My God is a mountain mover and a Giant slayer

- I can do all things through Jesus Christ who gives me strength

- I've been made more than a conqueror

- He that began a good work in me is able to perform it and finish it to the very end of my days

- I am blessed and highly favored

- I am the head and not the tail

- My God will supply all my needs

- My spirit is alive and Jesus lives in me

- I am living in the fullness of the Spirit

- My God will not fail me

- I am excited for each new day for every day holds new mercies and new opportunities.

- He will do what He said He would do

- I am Healthy, wealthy and wise

- I will live and not die and proclaim the works of the Lord

- I declare that my days will be long and I will inherit internal life

3. **Think win-win:** Have a win attitude: Like David when he faced Goliath. Look at this: He was in the Valley of Elah. Elah: means Shade. Shade hides the light. So, David was in a dark valley called Elah. Nev-

ertheless, let's take a look at the conversation with a win-win attitude that was full of faith:

1 Samuel 17:43-47

So the Philistine said to David, "Am I a dog, that you come to me with sticks?" And the Philistine cursed David by his gods. And the Philistine said to David, "Come to me, and I will give your flesh to the birds of the air and the beasts of the field!"

Then David said to the Philistine, "You come to me with a sword, with a spear, and with a javelin. But I come to you in the name of the Lord of hosts, the God of the armies of Israel, whom you have defied. **This day the Lord** *will deliver you into my hand, and I will strike you and take your head from you.* ***And this day*** *I will give the carcasses of the camp of the Philistines to the birds of the air and the wild beasts of the earth, that all the earth may know that there is a God in Israel. Then all this assembly shall know that the Lord does not save with sword and spear; for the battle is the Lord's, and He will give you into our hands."*

> When God writes upon your heart, He is not teasing you.
> He is serious about the plans He has for you.

David was in the Valley of Elah! He was in a low place, he was in darkness, he was surrounded by doubters, he was made fun of, and his own brothers were embarrassed by him and misunderstood his "FAITH IN GOD" for "haughtiness and pride."

There are 3 things that you must do every day and make them a part of who you are.

You have got to have an unshakeable Faith

1. You have to see the End from the Beginning and then WORK towards that goal. You cannot sit around and wait for something to happen. Put your faith in action!

2. You have got to have a positive attitude towards life and trials. You have to put your trust in God. You have to open the eyes of your heart and see HIM at work and then join HIM with what HE is doing.

3. What barriers are hindering you and the will of God in your life? Take time right now to Identify them.
    Then, by the power of Jesus Christ the Messiah, because He is:

    •   The One who "crossed over" from heaven to earth in the form of Man,

    •   The One who "crossed over" from life to death on the cross who bore all sin, all pain, all grief, all suffering, all shame and died death

    •   The One who "crossed over" from death to resurrecting life" who continues to give us life and who is always resurrecting dead things in our lives

    •   The One who "crossed over" from Earth to Heaven who is now seated at the right hand of the Father and He is making intercession for YOU right now

By the power of Jesus Christ and perfect sacrifice made on the cross, and because He is risen from the grave and right now He is at the right hand of the Father, interceding for You, He is cheering for you, so now begin crossing over from the "old" to the "new." You were born again to cross over. Now is the time to connect your faith with your dream. Believe God to fulfill every promise! Believe that HE will finish what HE starts in you.

Just as sure as He came, and He died, and He was raised from the dead and then ascended to the Father, He will come again. His promises are YES and Amen!

Jesus is praying for you to come UP higher to where He is. He has a seat saved for you! Just as He prayed for Peter in this manner in **Luke 22**, He is praying the same thing over you.

Luke 22:32 *(NKJV)*
*But I have prayed for you, that your __faith__ should not
fail; and when you have returned to Me, strengthen your
brethren."*

Here's the real question! What is Jesus praying for you? What are you
believing HIM for? What is being stirred up inside of you? Here is a very
personal question: Have you given up on the promise?

This is what Jesus is doing right now, He is praying for you that Your faith
will not fail you. He is praying you will never give up! He is asking you to
come UP and take a seat beside HIM and see from another perspective.
Not literally, but when you pray, take your imagination UP, prayers UP,
thoughts UP and get a Throne Room View so the eyes of your heart will be
enlightened.

Prayer:
Dear Jesus,
Thank You for Your love towards me. Thank you for the way You have
made me. Thank You for praying for me. Father, I ask You to help my
unbelief. I pray all my thoughts will begin to align with Your thoughts.
May the meditation of my heart be acceptable in Your sight. Lord, I have
a dream that You have placed in my heart. I want to move forward and
connect the resurrection power of faith to my dream that has died or been
put on a shelf. In Your perfect timing, I know that it will come to pass. But
while I wait, Lord show me what You want me to do. I pray for my ears to
have perfect pitch to your sweet voice. I don't want to miss what You are
saying. Lord, Your Word says that You will do above what I can even think,
imagine or comprehend! That means, if I can dream it, You can do it! Give
me creative ideas. Show me the will of heaven so I can walk it out here on
earth to the very ends of my days. I praise You for You will not leave me or
abandon me. You don't tease me with a dream, but You will fulfill all Your
promises for my life. I trust YOU! I love You, Jesus with all my heart. May
Your dreams become my dreams! In Jesus name I pray, Amen.

PERSONAL THOUGHTS

Day 21

Delayed Dreams

Jeremiah 29:11 *(NKJV)*
For I know the thoughts that I think toward you, says the Lord, thoughts of peace and not of evil, to give you a future and a hope.

God is writing the story of our life. He writes the plans that He has for us, but have you ever felt like your dreams are delayed, or put on hold? What is God up to? Why do I have to wait?

The real question is; if HE is writing my story, then what is He writing? What is He planning? What is God up to?

We see in the Bible the wonderful plans that HE had for Joseph, David, Daniel, Esther and Habakkuk, but what about for me?

Habakkuk 2:1-3 *(NIV)*

I want to bring out the key words in these verses.

1.   Write down the Revelation
2.   Position yourself to hear from God
3.   Keep your eyes open
4.   Make the revelation plain and clear as you write
5.   Run with it
6.   There is an appointed time
7.   It will NOT delay when the appointed time has come

It will not delay? Really? But I have felt like I have had dreams that have been delayed and even overlooked!

DELAYED DREAMS

Habakkuk 3:17-19

Though the fig tree <u>does not bud</u> and there are <u>no grapes on the vines</u>,

though the olive <u>crop fails</u> and the <u>fields produce no food</u>,

*though there are <u>no sheep in the pen</u> and **no cattle in the stalls**,*

*yet **I will rejoice in the Lord, I will be joyful in God my Savior**.*

*The Sovereign **Lord is my strength**; he makes my **feet like the feet of a deer, he enables me to tread on the heights**.*

What he's saying is, "In my contentment I have found the power to overcome, I have found strength to keep going, and somehow I have the energy to get through it."

What do I do when God writes a dream upon my heart and it has not come to pass and seems like it so far out of reach?

PAUL

Paul had a dream and a mandate. His dream was to get to Spain. He had a yearning and longing to get there. But along the way, his journey, he wrote a lot of good stuff and did a lot of amazing things.

Acts 19:21 *(NIV)*

he said, "I must visit Rome also."

Romans 15:20 *(NKJV)*

*And so I have **made it my aim to preach the gospel**, (His plan was to visit Rome)*

Romans 15:22-24,28

For this reason I also have been much hindered from coming to you. But now no longer having a place in these parts, and having a great desire these many years to come to you, whenever I journey to Spain, I shall come to you. For I hope to see you on my journey, and to be helped on my way there by you, if first I may enjoy your company for a while… Therefore, when I have performed this and have sealed to them this fruit, I shall go by way of you to Spain.

Paul's Plan was to GO to Spain, but he thought, while I am making my way to Spain, I will just preach the gospel everywhere I go.

> **Philippians 4:10-13 (NIV)**
> *I rejoiced greatly in the Lord that at last you renewed your concern for me. Indeed, you were concerned, but you had no opportunity to show it. I am not saying this because I am in need, for **I have learned to be content** whatever the circumstances. I know what it is to be in need, and I know what it is to have plenty. **I have learned the secret of being content in any and every situation**, whether well fed or hungry, whether living in plenty or in want. I can do all this through him who gives me strength."*

Paul made this statement while God was yet still writing dreams upon his heart. Maybe Paul was thinking what Hababbuk said in Chapter 3:17…

Lord, I am waiting and still believing and still praising you… even though my bank account is dried up, even though I am hungry, even though I am lonely, even though people have walked off and left me, even though my dreams seems so far away…
But Paul said:

> **I have learned to be content** whatever the circumstances.
> **I have learned the secret of being content in any and every situation.**

> **Being content is not a natural response;
> however, it is a learned behavior and it is a choice.**

What does Content mean:

In **Spanish** they use the word "Content" (contenta) for being Happy or satisfied or pleased.

Dictionary.com says content means: satisfied with what one is or has; not wanting more or anything else.

In Greek it means: self contained

BEING CONTENT IS LEARNED! THERE IS A SECRET IN CONTENTMENT! TO BE CONTENT DOES NOT MEAN TO SETTLE FOR LESS

Hebrews 13:5
Keep your lives free from the love of money and be **content (filled up with God)** *with what you have, because God has said, "Never will I leave you; never will I forsake you.*

1 Timothy 6:6
But godliness with **content***ment (self-contained, filled up with God) is great gain…*

1 Timothy 6:8
But if we have food and clothing, we will be **content** *(satisfied, happy, pleased) with that…*

Proverbs 19:23
The fear of the Lord leads to life; then one rests **content***, untouched by trouble.*

The secret of contentment is being untouched by trouble.

Being untouched by trouble is something we learn along the way.

Philippians 4
- *For I have learned to be "content" (stable, untouched by trouble, unshakeable, immovable, unchangeable) whatever the circumstances.*
- *I know what it is to be in need, and I know what it is to have plenty.*
- *I have learned the secret of being "content" stable, untouched by trouble, unshakeable, immovable, unchangeable) in any and every situation, whether well fed or hungry, whether living in plenty or in want.*

Then comes the famous line that we always quote:

> **"I can do all this through him (Jesus Christ) who gives me strength."**

Hababbuk said it like this:

He enables me to tread on the heights.

We know Paul went to Rome, and we know while he was in Rome he had intentions to go to Spain, but it is never recorded if he ever actually arrived at Spain. Some believe that He did, and some believe that he didn't.

Whether or not Paul ever went to Spain, regardless, God did more than Paul could ever think or imagine. God's dreams were bigger for Paul than his own. The reason he wanted to reach Spain is, so he could reach the world through Spain.

During the hardest times of his life, he learned what **Delayed Dreams** were all about, and he made a choice to be **CONTENT.** He decided either way, he was trusting God with the story line of his life and with his dream, even though it felt delayed. But it did not delay, the gospel has been preached and we have the inspired Word of God because Paul WROTE IT DOWN as God spoke.

Now, it is time for you to write it down. It may feel like it's delayed, but it's not been forgotten and God has a perfect timing.

Maybe you are like Habakkuk in Chapter 2...

1. You have Written down the Revelation
2. You have Positioned yourself to hear from God
3. You have Kept your eyes open
4. You have made the revelation plain and clear
5. You've been running with it by putting action with your faith
6. Like Joseph, David, Esther, Daniel, Habakkuk, Like Paul...
7. There is an appointed time
8. It will NOT delay when the appointed time has come

IT WILL COME TO PASS!

Prayer:

Dear Lord,

I come before Your Throne Room of Grace, presenting to You my heart. For in my heart flows the issues of life. Every problem I have, and every doubt I have comes from my heart. I ask You to touch my heart and to put together the broken pieces of my life. I seek Your face and Your will. I just want more of You in my life. Lord, every day I seek You and acknowledge that I need You more with every breath I breathe. More than the air I breathe, more than the song I sing, more than the next heartbeat, Lord, I need You more than anything.

As Moses said in *Exodus 33:13-16*

> *"If it is true that you look favorably on me, let me know your ways so I may understand you more fully and continue to enjoy your favor. And remember that this nation is your very own people."*

The Lord replied, "I will personally go with you, Moses, and I will give you rest—everything will be fine for you."

Then Moses said, "If you don't personally go with us, don't make us leave this place. How will anyone know that you look favorably on me—on me and on your people—if you don't go with us? For your presence among us sets your people and me apart from all other people on the earth."

Fulfill Your promises in me like You did in Moses. How will people know my Lord if You don't go before me and map the way out for me? MY Lord, I will follow You wherever You go. Let Your will be done here on earth as it is in Heaven for my life and for my dreams. I ask this all in Your name Jesus. I come to Your Throne Room to ask heaven to move. Show me Your glory, and Your face. Reveal Yourself to me. Amen!

PERSONAL THOUGHTS

A Letter From Jesus

To My Beloved Sons and Daughters,

As I have told you before, I will do even more and more abundantly than you could ever ask or imagine. My plans for you are so good! And My thoughts for you outnumber the sands of the sea. My heart is drawn towards you and My eyes are set on you. It is My great desire to bless you.

Be strong and courageous. In this next chapter of your life. Spend your life LIVING and not dying! To worry is to die, but to trust is to live. To control in fear is to die, but to let go in love give you the freedom to LIVE!

You have many emotions right now because your spirit senses what is ahead, and your soul is overwhelmed. But remember, when you heart fails you, I am bigger than your heart. I will never leave you and I will never fail you. My heart is tender towards you. My intentions are kind and yet My love is more powerful than a hurricane. My love is wetter than rain. My love is smoother than oil.

I am revealing My heart to you and it will shatter your counterfeit foundation! Like an earth quake, I will swallow up what is fake. I have chosen you as much as anybody. I have heard your request you have made known to Me. My sons and daughters, why do you limit Me? I am ready to show the church what I am capable of! I know you are scared. So, trust Me.

Give up your rights to be afraid. Give up your rights to be sick. Give up your rights to be depressed and discouraged. Give up your rights to be financially bound. Give up your rights to worry.

My love will not only wash you clean of all your sin, guilt and shame, but My love will sustain you, My love will promote you. My love will push you to higher heights. I will cause you to dream again!

You have the right to be called sons and daughters of the King. You have the right to be healthy. You have the right to be courageous and bold. You have the right to walk in My JOY. You have the right to have financial freedom. You have the right to trust Me with your life. You have the right to be prosperous, in your spirit, soul and body.

Now is the time to give up all your negative thoughts and trade them in for the TRUTH. My Word is powerful, and it is true. By real faith in Me, My blessings will be released but doubt will hinder it.

Change is coming! Not only in your house, but in My church, and in the World. I am coming soon!

Don't forget your purpose and your destination. You were placed here for a specific purpose and your life matters!

TRUST ME WITH YOUR LIFE!

TRUST ME WITH YOUR CHILDREN!

TRUST ME WITH YOUR SPOUSE!

TRUST ME WITH YOUR DESTINY!

Right now, I am at work behind the scenes! Get ready for change as you learn to come to Me in the Throne Room. Get ready to be renewed in your mind! I am HE who is interceding for you and WHO is writing your story. Be at peace with the pages of your life as I am working all things together for your good. I am in search of whose heart is open to receive from Me. Come to Me and you will find rest for your weary soul.

I LOVE YOU SO MUCH!

Love,
Jesus

About the Author

Janet Swanson is the worship pastor at CrossRoads Community Church where her husband, Cary is the Senior Pastor. Janet and Cary have been married since August 19, 1989 and have three sons (Reed, Rhett, and Ryan). Her family is her total devotion and is her greatest passion.

Janet has been involved in ministry since 1988 and served faithfully in full time ministry in the Church of God (Cleveland, TN) since 1999. She is an ordained minister.

Janet sings, leads worship and composes music. She is the author of One Voice and has recently devoted a healing and prayer CD "Near to the Broken" to those who are grieving or experiencing loss of any kind.

Spanish and Spanish-speaking people are dear to **Janet's** heart. She has dedicated much time and effort to achieve fluency in Spanish. She has a strong desire to see people in relationship with the Lord Jesus Christ that will lead to total victory, every time, in every situation.

Personal time with the Lord is the single most influential factor in the success and significance of **Janet's** life and ministry. Her greatest satisfaction in ministry is when she is anointed to lead people into God's presence for salvation, healing and deliverance.

Janet has a strong prophetic anointing, which is especially manifested as she ministers in music.

For more information on
Janet Swanson and Resources,
call 912-764-4539,
email janetswansonministries@gmail.com,
or visit www.janetswansonministries.org.

References

The Book of Mysteries, by Jonathan Cahn, FrontLine, 2016.

All Bible references were researched and cited using:
"BibleGateway." - - Bible Gateway, www.biblegateway.com/.

Amplified Bible (AMP).
   Copyright © 2015 by The Lockman Foundation, La Habra, CA 90631.

Amplified Bible, Classic Edition (AMPC).
   Copyright © 1954, 1958, 1962, 1964, 1965, 1987 by The Lockman Foundation

English Standard Version® (ESV). Text Edition: 2016.
   Copyright © 2001 by Crossway Bibles, a publishing ministry of Good News Publishers.

King James Version (KJV). Public Domain

New American Standard Bible (NASB).
   Copyright © 1960, 1962, 1963, 1968, 1971, 1972, 1973, 1975, 1977, 1995
   by The Lockman Foundation

New International Version (NIV).
   Copyright © 1973, 1978, 1984, 2011 by Biblica

New King James Version® (NKJV).
   Copyright © 1982 by Thomas Nelson.

New Life Version (NLV)
   Copyright © 1969 by Christian Literature International

New Living Translation (NLT).
   Copyright © 1996, 2004, 2015 by Tyndale House Foundation.

The Living Bible (TLB).
   Copyright © 1971 by Tyndale House Foundation.

The Message (MSG).
   Copyright © 1993, 1994, 1995, 1996, 2000, 2001, 2002 by Eugene H. Peterson